W9-API-023

**Designed**

*to* *Inspire!*

*to* *Encourage!*

*to* *Motivate!*

# THE GREAT BOOK OF
# INSPIRING QUOTATIONS

## Motivational Sayings For All Occasions

Compiled by

Dr. Peter Klavora
**University of Toronto**

Dr. Dave Chambers
**York University**

Sport Books Publisher

**Canadian Cataloguing in Publication Data**

Klavora, Peter
   **The great book of inspiring quotations: Motivational sayings for all occasions**

ISBN 0-920905-64-1

1. Inspiration – Quotations, maxims, etc. 2. Sports – Psychological aspects – Quotations, maxims, etc. 3. Success in business – Quotations, maxims, etc. I. Chambers, Dave, 1940-. II. Title.


PN6081.k52 2001                  081                  C00-932253-1

Distribution world-wide by
Sport Books Publisher


http://www.sportbookspub.com
E-mail: sbp@sportbookspub.com
Fax: 416-966-9022


Printed in the United States

# Dedication

To the many coaches who inspire their athletes to reach their full potential.

To business leaders who motivate their co-workers to reach their goals.

To all those who strive to grow through personal study and reflection.

# Preface

This book represents the result of years of industrious collecting. The quotations gathered here are international in scope and have a wide chronological range, from ancient to contemporary. The selection draws on a variety of sources and authors, from philosophers and poets to athletes, coaches, and executives. We have made every effort to trace the authorship of all quotations, although some of them remain anonymous.

The collection is arranged under thirty-one motivational and inspirational headings. Although few of the sayings we have included can be restricted to a single category, each in fact appears only once under the heading we considered the most useful or pertinent.

Our goal throughout has been simple: to inspire, motivate, and encourage readers. We hope this volume will not only serve speakers and leaders in sport, business, and indeed many other fields, as a useful source for all occasions, but also prove a welcome personal source for study and reflection.

# Contents

# *Ability*

$W$hat we must decide is perhaps how we are valuable rather than how valuable we are.
EDGAR Z. FRIEDENBERG

$C$ertain sports are made for certain people— every athlete must find the sport for which he or she is best suited.
BILLIE JEAN KING

$N$o matter what the level of ability, you have more potential than you can ever develop in a lifetime.
JAMES T. McCAY

$A$n idea is only as good as its execution.
ANONYMOUS

$T$here is nothing more unequal than the equal treatment of unequals.
KEN BLANCHARD

$T$o do easily what is difficult for others is the mark of talent. To do what is impossible for talent is the mark of genius.
HENRI FRÉDÉRIC AMIEL

It's hard for truly great players to understand how difficult the game is for players with less ability than they themselves have.
DEL HARRIS

A man must not deny his manifest abilities, for that is to evade his obligations.
ROBERT LOUIS STEVENSON

It is always pleasant to be urged to do something on the ground that one can do it well.
GEORGE SANTAYANA

The winds and waves are always on the side of the ablest navigators.
EDWARD GIBBON

Do the very best you can with what you have.
THEODORE ROOSEVELT

Regardless of what you do put in, every game boils down to doing the things you do best, and doing them over and over again.
ANONYMOUS

# Ability

Intelligence is quickness to apprehend as distinct from ability, which is capacity to act wisely on the thing apprehended.
ALFRED NORTH WHITEHEAD

When two do the same thing it is never quite the same thing.
PUBLILIUS SYRUS

Don't measure what you should have accomplished with your ability.
JOHN WOODEN

It is a great ability to be able to conceal one's ability.
FRANÇOIS DE LA ROCHEFOUCAULD

Good pitching will always stop good hitting, and vice versa.
CASEY STENGEL

In a world as empirical as ours, a youngster who does not know what he is good *at* will not be sure what he is good *for*.
EDGAR Z. FRIEDENBERG

Everyone must row with the oars he has.
ENGLISH PROVERB

The barrier between success is not something which exists in the real world; it is composed purely and simply of doubts about ability.
MARK CAINE

A man is what he does and does well. That's one thing I learned in my life.
ELIA KAZAN

A really great talent finds its happiness in execution.
JOHANN WOLFGANG VON GOETHE

Men are born equal but they are also born different.
ERICH FROMM

There is hardly anybody good for everything, and there is scarcely anybody who is absolutely good for nothing.
LORD CHESTERFIELD

# *Attitude*

Things turn out best for the people who make the best of the way things turn out.
JOHN WOODEN

No one can make you feel inferior without your consent.
ELEANOR ROOSEVELT

If you make every game a life-and-death proposition, you're going to have problems. For one thing, you'll be dead a lot.
DEAN SMITH

The most important ingredient in your gym bag is your attitude.
ANONYMOUS

Where he falls short, 'tis Nature's fault alone;
Where he succeeds, the merit's all his own.
CHARLES CHURCHILL

Most of us are satisfied with so little in ourselves but demand so much from others.
ANONYMOUS

I am willing to admit I may not always be right, but I am never wrong.
SAMUEL GOLDWYN


Remember, you meet your opponents, not their reputations.
ANONYMOUS


Everyone of us always acts, feels, and behaves in a way that is consistent with our self-image—regardless of the reality of that image.
PSYCHO-CYBER 2000


It is not the weight of the load that gets you down, it's the way you carry it.
ANONYMOUS


Men are not prisoners of fate, but only prisoners of their own minds.
FRANKLIN D. ROOSEVELT


Creative minds are like parachutes… they work only when they are open.
ANONYMOUS

# *Attitude*

**P**ride is a personal commitment. It is an attitude that separates excellence from mediocrity.
ANONYMOUS

**I**t's not the situation… it's your reaction to the situation.
BOB CONKLIN

**H**ow we think shows through in how we act. Attitudes are mirrors of the mind. They reflect thinking.
DAVID JOSEPH SCHWARTZ

**Y**our attitude tells the world what you expect from life and whether you will achieve it or not.
ANONYMOUS

**A** man is not hurt so much by what happens, as by his opinion of what happens.
MICHEL EYQUEM MONTAIGNE

**I**f you can't change your fate, change your attitude.
AMY TAN

All you need is to tell a man that he is no good ten times a day, and very soon he begins to believe it himself.
LIN YUTANG

Whether you think you can or think you can't—you are right.
HENRY FORD

The minute you get the idea you're indispensable, you aren't.
ANONYMOUS

I will never be an old man. To me, old age is always fifteen years older than I am.
BERNARD M. BARUCH

A positive attitude is not a destination – it's a way of life.
ANONYMOUS

I don't believe in failure. It is not failure if you enjoyed the process.
OPRAH WINFREY

# *Attitude*

**T**ake your job seriously, not yourself.
NEWT GINGRICH

**B**reak free by changing your perspective.
ANONYMOUS

**A**ttitude is an inner concept. It is the most important thing you can develop in your life.
WAYNE DYER

**M**ental toughness is essential to success.
VINCE LOMBARDI

**D**on't take life too seriously… nobody gets out alive anyway.
ANONYMOUS

**I**ntellect will only take you as far as your attitude will allow.
TIM PAULEY

**T**he right attitude and one arm will beat the wrong attitude and two arms every time.
ANONYMOUS

We can do only what we think we can do. We can be only what we think we can be. We can have only what we think we can have. What we do, what we are, what we have, all depend upon what we think.
ROBERT COLLIER

Attitude is a little thing that makes a big difference.
ANONYMOUS

Keep your face to the sunshine and you cannot see the shadows.
HELEN KELLER

A man does not stay defeated because of something that happens to him, but within him.
ANONYMOUS

The first and most important step toward success is the feeling that we can succeed.
NELSON BOSWELL

Your attitude will determine your altitude.
ANONYMOUS

# *Attitude*

**O**ur life is what our thoughts make it.
MARCUS AURELIUS ANTONINUS

**A**ge is a question of mind over matter. If you don't mind, it doesn't matter.
SATCHEL PAGE

**L**iving on earth is expensive, but at least you get a free trip around the sun.
ANONYMOUS

**L**ife is 10% what happens to me and 90% how I react to it.
LOU HOLTZ

**L**eadership is an attitude before it is an ability.
ANONYMOUS

**B**eauty is in the eye of the beholder.
MARGARET WOLFE HUNGERFORD

**A** man is literally what he thinks.
JAMES ALLEN

It is more important than appearance, giftedness, or skill. It will make or break a company… a home… a team. The remarkable thing is we have a choice every day regarding the ATTITUDE we will embrace for that day. We cannot change our past, we cannot change the inevitable, but we can change our ATTITUDE.
ANONYMOUS

Negative attitudes are a sort of poison.
FRAN TARKENTON

A mind free of negatives produces positives. I think victory, I get victory.
ANONYMOUS

If you accept losing, you can't win.
VINCE LOMBARDI

Attitudes are contagious. Is yours worth catching?
ANONYMOUS

# Belief

All things are possible to one who believes.
SAINT BERNARD OF CLAIRVAUX

I don't think anything is unrealistic if you
believe you can do it.
MIKE DITKA

What you believe yourself to be, you are.
CLAUDE M. BRISTOL

There is nothing on earth you cannot have,
once you have mentally accepted the fact that you
can have it.
ROBERT COLLIER

He can who thinks he can, and he can't who
thinks he can't. This is an inexorable, indisputable
law.
ORISON SWETT MARDEN

Nothing splendid has ever been achieved
except by those who dared believe that something
inside of them was superior to circumstance.
BRUCE BARTON

No man is happy unless he believes he is.
PUBLILIUS SYRUS


Faith is the quality or power by which the things desired become the things possessed.
KATHRYN KUHLMAN


All the strength and force of man comes from his faith in things unseen. He who believes is strong; he who doubts is weak. Strong convictions precede great actions.
JAMES F. CLARKE


If you think you can, you can. And if you think you can't, you're right.
MARY KAY ASH


Faith is to believe what you do not yet see; the reward for this faith is to see what you believe.
SAINT AUGUSTINE


There is nothing either good or bad, but thinking makes it so.
WILLIAM SHAKESPEARE

# Belief

To believe with certainty, we must begin with doubting.
STANISLAS I, KING OF POLAND

To be a champ you have to believe in yourself when nobody else will.
SUGAR RAY ROBINSON

Life's battles don't always go to the stronger or faster man, but sooner or later the man who wins is the fellow who thinks he can.
ANONYMOUS

They are able because they think they are able.
VIRGIL

The man who believes he can do something is probably right, and so is the man who believes he can't.
ANDREW JACKSON

A man lives by believing something; not by debating and arguing about many things.
THOMAS CARLYLE

Believe that life *is* worth living, and your belief will help create the fact.
WILLIAM JAMES

Faith is believing in what you know ain't so.
MARK TWAIN

I could find the determination to keep on going. I learned that your mind can amaze your body, if you just keep telling yourself, I can do it, I can do it.
JON ERICKSON

It is believing in roses that one brings them to bloom.
FRENCH PROVERB

The things always happen that you really believe in; and the belief in a thing makes it happen.
FRANK LLOYD WRIGHT

# Challenge

If it had not been for the wind in my face, I wouldn't be able to fly at all.
ARTHUR ASHE

When people keep telling you that you can't do a thing, you kind of like to try it.
MARGARET CHASE SMITH

Change is not made without inconvenience, even from worse to better.
RICHARD HOOKER

Unless you try to do something beyond what you have already done and mastered, you will never grow.
ANONYMOUS

Errors, like straws, upon the surface flow; He who would search for pearls must dive below.
JOHN DRYDEN

If everything is going your way, you are probably heading in the wrong direction.
ANONYMOUS

Fire is the test of gold; adversity, of strong men.
LUCIUS ANNAEUS SENECA

Your biggest task is not to get ahead of others, but to surpass yourself.
ANONYMOUS

The great pleasure in life is doing what people say you cannot do.
WALTER BAGEHOT

The normal reaction to an idea is to think of reasons why it cannot be done.
ANONYMOUS

The more success one achieves, the more pressure there is that goes with it, and I accept it. I'd sure rather have the pressure of success than the lack of pressure that goes with anonymity.
ROGER CLEMENS

One day you are drinking the wine, and the next day you are picking the grapes.
LOU HOLTZ

# Challenge

It is difficulties that show what men are.
EPICTETUS

Adversity is the state in which a man most easily becomes acquainted with himself….
SAMUEL JOHNSON

The tougher the job, the greater the reward.
ANONYMOUS

That which does not kill me makes me stronger.
FRIEDRICH WILHELM NIETZSCHE

Defeat must be faced, but it need not be final.
ANONYMOUS

Never was good work done without trouble.
CHINESE PROVERB

We accomplish in proportion to what we attempt.
ANONYMOUS

Becoming number one is easier than remaining number one.
BILL BRADLEY

Not only do many people 'want their cake and eat it, too,' they also want your cake.
ANONYMOUS

I've never known anybody to achieve anything without overcoming adversity.
LOU HOLTZ

To achieve all that is possible, we must attempt the impossible.
ANONYMOUS

One of the great discoveries a man makes, one of his greatest surprises, is to find he can do what he was afraid he couldn't do.
HENRY FORD

Nobody said life would be easy… and you only make it tougher if you feel sorry for yourself.
MORLEY FRASER

# Challenge

The wind blows the strongest upon those who stand the tallest.
F. C. HAYES

The impossible is what nobody can do until someone does it.
ANONYMOUS

It is all too easy to become focused on yesterday's success rather than today's challenges.
JAMES A. BELASCO AND RALPH C. STAYER

By having adversity in life we can see in others and in ourselves who quits and those who won't quit; and in the end, adversity will make winners of those who won't quit.
ANONYMOUS

Accept that some days you're the pigeon, and some days you're the statue.
SCOTT ADAMS

Every great achievement once seemed impossible.
ANONYMOUS

Whilst he sits on the cushion of advantages he goes to sleep. When pushed, tormented, defeated, he has a chance to learn something.
RALPH WALDO EMERSON

Do not fear the winds of adversity. Remember, a kite rises against the wind rather than with it.
ANONYMOUS

Every noble work is at first impossible.
THOMAS CARLYLE

Adversity makes some people break and makes others break records.
ANONYMOUS

If you're not just a little bit nervous before a match, you probably don't have the expectations of yourself that you should have.
HALE IRWIN

Be thankful for adversity—it separates the winners from the quitters.
ANONYMOUS

Challenges can be stepping stones or stumbling blocks. It's just a matter of how you view them.
ANONYMOUS

Tackle your hardest job first. Usually when we are faced with a number of projects to work on, we take the easiest or the most rewarding one first. Start with a job you really don't want to do. Once you get it out of the way, everything else will seem easy.
RED AUERBACH

Accept the challenges so that you may feel the exhilaration of victory.
ANONYMOUS

No matter how long you have been playing, you still feel the butterflies before the big ones.
PEE WEE REESE

Often times the roughest road may be the best way to get where you want to go.
ANONYMOUS

Without a risk there can be no challenge; without challenge there can be no reward.
DAVE MANCUSO

Despair doubles our strength.
JOHN RAY

It is easier to become a champion than to stay a champion.
ANONYMOUS

Happiness is beneficial for the body, but it is grief that develops the powers of the mind.
MARCEL PROUST

When things go wrong, as they sometimes will, when the road you're trudging seems all uphill; when the funds are low and the debts are high, and you want to smile but you have to sigh; when life is pressing you down a bit – rest if you must, but don't you quit.
ANONYMOUS

# Character

The measure of a person's real character is what they would do if they knew they would never be found out.
THOMAS MACAULEY

Talent will get you to the top, but it takes character to keep you there.
JOHN WOODEN

The true perfection of man lies not in what man has, but in what man is.
OSCAR WILDE

No price is too high to pay for a good reputation.
ANONYMOUS

The truth about a man lies first and foremost in what he hides.
ANDRÉ MALRAUX

Sow an act, and you reap a habit. Sow a habit, and you reap a character. Sow a character, and you reap a destiny.
CHARLES READE

It is easier to fight for one's principles than to live up to them.
ALFRED ADLER

Don't belittle… be big.
ANONYMOUS

The greatest of faults, I should say, is to be conscious of none.
THOMAS CARLYLE

When we seek to discover the best in others, we somehow bring out the best in ourselves.
WILLIAM ARTHUR WARD

The cream rises to the top, but so does scum.
ANONYMOUS

Our deeds determine us, as much as we determine our needs.
GEORGE ELIOT

We boil at different degrees.
RALPH WALDO EMERSON

# Character

$F$ollow the three R's:
- Respect for self;
- Respect for others; and
- Responsibility for all your actions.
ANONYMOUS

$C$haracter equals destiny.
HERACLITUS

$I$t matters not how a man dies, but how he lives.
SAMUEL JOHNSON

$F$ollowing the path of least resistance is what makes rivers and men crooked.
ANONYMOUS

$N$obody holds a good opinion of a man who has a low opinion of himself.
ANTHONY TROLLOPE

$A$ man should *be* upright, not be *kept* upright.
MARCUS AURELIUS ANTONINUS

When a man is wrapped up in himself, he makes a pretty small package.
ANONYMOUS

Every man has three characters: that which he exhibits, that which he has, and that which he thinks he has.
ALPHONSE KARR

A sound body is good; a sound mind is better; but a strong and clean character is better than either.
THEODORE ROOSEVELT

If we would create something, we must be something.
ANONYMOUS

Character is much easier kept than recovered.
THOMAS PAINE

We are all alike…. The difference is the heart.
ANONYMOUS

# Character

The higher we are placed, the more we should be humble.
MARCUS TULLIUS CICERO

I don't want any yes-men around me. I want everybody to tell me the truth even if it costs them their jobs.
SAMUEL GOLDWYN

Character consists of what you do on the third and fourth tries.
ANONYMOUS

If you can't stand the heat, get out of the kitchen.
HARRY S. TRUMAN

To keep your character intact you cannot stoop to filthy acts. It makes it easier to stoop the next time.
KATHERINE HEPBURN

To get the true measure of a man, note how much more he does than is required of him.
ANONYMOUS

The true test of character is not how much we know how to do, but how we behave when we don't know what to do.
JOHN HOLT

Try not to become a man of success but rather try to become a man of value.
ALBERT EINSTEIN

There is no right way to do the wrong thing.
ANONYMOUS

In matters of principle, stand like a rock; in matters of taste, swim with the current.
THOMAS JEFFERSON

True grit is making a decision and standing by it, doing what must be done – for no moral man can have peace of mind if he leaves undone what he knows he should have done.
JOHN WAYNE

One cannot always be a hero, but one can always be a man.
ANONYMOUS

Character

In the arena of human life, the honours and rewards fall to those who show their good qualities in action.
ARISTOTLE

Class is an intangible quality which commands, rather than demands, the respect of others.
JOHN WOODEN

Win without boasting, lose without excuse.
ALBERT PAYSON TERHUNE

The one who complains about the way the ball bounces is likely the one who dropped it.
ANONYMOUS

Genius is formed in quiet, character in the stream of human life.
JOHANN WOLFGANG VON GOETHE

You can tell more about a person by what he says about others… than you can by what others say about him.
ANONYMOUS

If we are strong, our character will speak for itself. If we are weak, words will be of no help.
JOHN F. KENNEDY

The bigger a man's head gets, the easier it is to fill his shoes.
ANONYMOUS

Pride… character… work habits… lead to success.
RICK COMELY

Character is like a tree and reputation like its shadow. The shadow is what we think of it; the tree is the real thing.
ABRAHAM LINCOLN

Before you flare up at anyone's faults, take time to count ten, ten of your own.
ANONYMOUS

A man who doesn't stand for something will fall for anything.
PETER MARSHALL

# *Character*

Character is a conquest, not a bequest.
ANONYMOUS

We make a living by what we get; we make a life by what we give.
W. A. NANCE

The people most preoccupied with titles and status are usually the least deserving of them.
ANONYMOUS

A man's reputation is the opinion people have of him, his character is what he really is.
JACK MINER

What counts is not the size of the dog in the fight, but the size of the fight in the dog.
DWIGHT D. EISENHOWER

The test of any man lies in action.
PINDAR

Macho does not prove mucho.
ANONYMOUS

**K**indness can become its own motive. We are made kind by being kind.
ERIC HOFFER

**I**t is no disgrace to fail, but to lie there and grunt is.
ANONYMOUS

**W**aste no time arguing what a good man should be. Be one.
MARCUS AURELIUS ANTONINUS

**I**t isn't the plays or the system that gets the job done, it's the quality of the people in the system.
JOE PATERNO

**I**f you do the right thing every time you will please the most people, and astonish others.
ANONYMOUS

**T**hough intelligence is powerless to modify character, it is a dab hand at finding euphemisms for its weakness.
QUENTIN CRISP

# Character

The best kind of pride is that which compels a man to do his very best work, even if no one is watching.
ANONYMOUS

A team that has character does not need stimulation.
TOM LANDRY

Why do you have to lose to prove you are a good sport?
ANONYMOUS

Success without honour is an unseasoned dish; it will satisfy your hunger, but it won't taste good.
JOE PATERNO

When the going gets tough, the tough get going.
ANONYMOUS

Character is made by what you stand for; reputation, by what you fall for.
ROBERT QUILLEN

People usually get at odds with each other when they try to get even.
ANONYMOUS

He who is good for making excuses is seldom good for anything else.
BENJAMIN FRANKLIN

Winning without arrogance, losing without alibi.
GRANTLAND RICE

When a winner makes a mistake, he says, "I was wrong." When a loser makes a mistake, he says, "It was not my fault."
ANONYMOUS

Conscience is the inner voice which warns us that someone may be looking.
H. L. MENCKEN

Be humble—a lot was accomplished before you were born.
ANONYMOUS

Bad language promotes poor sportsmanship.
KENNETH KLADNIK

It's not hard to make decisions when you know what your values are.
ANONYMOUS

Those who are upset by criticism admit they deserve it.
CORNELIUS TACITUS

Hard work spotlights the character of people: some turn up their sleeves, some turn up their noses, and some don't turn up at all.
SAM EWIG

Success, like self-worth, is something that must be determined by each individual according to the standards, beliefs, and values that they use to guide their life.
JOHN WOODEN

What lies behind us and what lies before us are tiny matters compared to what lies within us.
RALPH WALDO EMERSON

Enter the game a gentleman – exit the same way.
ANONYMOUS

A man may make mistakes, but he isn't a failure until he starts blaming someone else.
JOHN WOODEN

Some men succeed by what they know; some by what they do; and a few by what they are.
ELBERT HUBBARD

There are certain qualities that you look for in people, whether you are on a football team or in business. You look for people who are committed, devoted, and doing the best job. Talent isn't going to matter either. I'll take the guy who is out breaking his butt over a guy with talent in a close situation every time. I may get my butt beat a few times, but in the long run, I'll win because I'll have a guy with more character.
MIKE DITKA

When you lose, say little. When you win, say less.
ANONYMOUS

# Character

Your character is defined by your actions, not merely by your thought. Your actions represent who you are, while your thoughts only represent what you would like to be.

ANONYMOUS

Another team can be beating you for six innings, but for some reason the good ball teams get tough and win them in the last three.

BILLY MARTIN

The stupidest thing in the world is a man with his own gifts trying to act like someone else. You can be taught and you can be inspired, but you've still got to be you.

WILLIE MAYS

One can acquire everything in solitude— except character.

STENDHAL

The ultimate measure of a man is not where he stands in moments of comfort and convenience, but where he stands at times of challenge and controversy.

MARTIN LUTHER KING

A winner never whines.

PAUL BROWN

Open your arms to change, but don't let go of your values.

ANONYMOUS

Character is what you know you are, not what others think you have.

MARVA COLLINS

There is never a better measure of what a person is than what he does when he is absolutely free to choose.

WILLIAM M. BULGER

The applause soon dies away, the prize is left behind, but the character you build up is yours forever.

ANONYMOUS

Nearly all men can stand adversity, but if you want to test a man's character, give him power.

ABRAHAM LINCOLN

# Commitment

I'm not just involved in tennis but committed. Do you know the difference between involvement and commitment? Think of ham and eggs. The chicken is involved. The pig is committed.
MARTINA NAVRATILOVA

In winning, total commitment is necessary.
JEFF DAVIS

He who considers his work beneath him will be above doing it well.
ALEXANDER CHASE

Winners are men who have dedicated their lives to winning.
ANONYMOUS

The only immorality is to not do what one has to do when one has to do it.
JEAN ANOUILH

Success is not a sometimes thing. In other words, you don't do what is right once in awhile, but all the time. Success is a habit. Winning is a habit.
VINCE LOMBARDI

Authority has every reason to fear the skeptic, for authority can rarely survive in the face of doubt.
ROBERT LINDNER

Duty is what one expects of others, it is not what one does oneself.
OSCAR WILDE

A winner makes commitments, a loser makes promises.
ANONYMOUS

Football requires a certain amount of Spartanism. It requires great sacrifice and self-denial and you must have control of yourself.
VINCE LOMBARDI

Productivity comes from commitment, not from authority.
W. L. GORE

Lawful and settled authority is very seldom resisted when it is well employed.
SAMUEL JOHNSON

# Commitment

Some people are as reliable as the sunrise.
ANONYMOUS

It's the law of the harvest. You plant the seed, you water the seed, you fertilize the seed, and you weed the seed. If you do those things, and only if you do them, you will harvest.
REYNOLD GARDNER

Giving up reinforces a sense of incompetence. Going on gives you a commitment to succeed.
ANONYMOUS

Eighty percent of success is showing up.
WOODY ALLEN

It is our responsibilities, not ourselves, that we should take seriously.
PETER USTINOV

No horse gets anywhere till he is harnessed. No stream ever drives anything until it is confined. No life grows until it is focused, dedicated, and disciplined.
ANONYMOUS

You must dedicate yourself to a far-reaching goal and sacrifice to reach it. You must enjoy what you do. Reach beyond your abilities; recognize that no talent, without hard work, can make you a winner.
GEORGE ALLEN

Whatever you do, don't do it halfway.
BOB BEAMON

It's all about getting good people—people who believe in what we're doing.
MIKE KRZYZEWSKI

We want men who will stand up and be counted for. Men who will make something happen.
JERRY GLANVILLE

The duration of an athletic contest is only a few minutes, while the training for it takes weeks of arduous work and continuous exercise of self-effort.
ANONYMOUS

# Concentration

Concentrate… for the greatest achievements are reserved for the man of single aim, in whom no rival powers divide the empire of the soul.
ORISON SWETT MARDEN

I just try to concentrate on concentrating.
MARTINA NAVRATILOVA

Concentrate all your thoughts upon the work at hand. The sun's rays do not burn until brought to a focus.
ALEXANDER GRAHAM BELL

Everyone has a photographic memory. Some don't have film.
ANONYMOUS

A preoccupation with the future not only prevents us from seeing the present as it is, but often prompts us to rearrange the past.
ERIC HOFFER

The most important thing in communication is to hear what isn't being said.
PETER F. DRUCKER

All the problems of the world are caused by people who do not listen.
FRANCO ZEFFIRELLI

What do I mean by concentration? I mean focusing totally on the business at hand and commanding your body to do exactly what you want it to do.
ARNOLD PALMER

Concentrate all your thoughts on the great desire in your life. This concentration must be continuous, unceasing – every minute, every hour, every day, every week.
CHARLES E. POPPLESTONE

Concentrate on one thing at a time, and rule out all outside influences that don't have any real bearing on the task at hand.
MARTY LIQUORI

When you walk out on the court, clear your mind of everything unrelated to the goal of playing the match as well as you can.
STAN SMITH

# Concentration

Concentrate… put all your eggs in one basket, and watch that basket….
ANDREW CARNEGIE

As every divided kingdom falls, so every mind divided between many studies confounds and saps itself.
LEONARDO DA VINCI

I'm so broke I can't even pay attention.
ANONYMOUS

I always know what's happening on the court. I see a situation occur, and I respond.
LARRY BIRD

If you've got to remind yourself to concentrate during competition, you've got no chance to concentrate.
BOBBY NICHOLS

Concentration, in its truest, unadulterated form, means being able to focus the mind on one single solitary thing.
KOMAR

You can do only one thing at a time.... I simply tackle one problem and concentrate all efforts on what I am doing at the moment.
MAXWELL MALTZ

The weakest living creature, by concentrating his powers on a single object, can accomplish something; whereas the strongest, by dispersing his over many, may fail to accomplish anything.
THOMAS CARLYLE

There is no job so simple that it cannot be done wrong.
ANONYMOUS

Concentrate on finding your goal, then concentrate on reaching it.
COL M. FRIEDSAM

# Confidence

**S**elf-confidence is the first requisite to great undertakings.
SAMUEL JOHNSON

**E**xperience tells you what to do; confidence allows you to do it.
STAN SMITH

**K**ill the snake of doubt in your soul, crush the worms of fear in your heart, and mountains will move out of your way.
KATE SEREDY

**E**rror has never even come close to my mind.
PRINCE CLEMENT METTERNICH

**M**ake your opponent fear and respect you.
KNUTE ROCKNE

**N**othing gives one person so much advantage over another as to remain always cool and unruffled under all circumstances.
THOMAS JEFFERSON

They can do all because they think they can.
VIRGIL

When you have confidence, you can have a lot of fun; and when you have fun, you can do amazing things.
JOE NAMATH

He didn't know it couldn't be done… so he did it.
ANONYMOUS

You've got to take the initiative and play your game…. Confidence makes the difference.
CHRIS EVERT

If you're prepared, then you're able to feel confident.
ROBERT J. RINGER

There can be no great courage where there is no confidence or assurance, and half the battle is in the conviction that we can do what we undertake.
ORISON SWETT MARDEN

# Confidence

Every great hitter works on the theory that the pitcher is more afraid of him than he is of the pitcher.
TY COBB

One important key to success is self-confidence. An important key to self-confidence is preparation.
ARTHUR ASHE

Besides pride, loyalty, discipline, heart, and mind, confidence is the key to all the locks.
JOE PATERNO

I never quit trying. I never felt that I didn't have a chance to win.
ARNOLD PALMER

Never bend your head, always hold it high. Look the world straight in the face.
HELEN KELLER

Winning breeds confidence, and confidence breeds winning.
HUBERT GREEN

Confidence is the result of hours and days and weeks and years of constant work and dedication.
ROGER STAUBACH

As is our confidence, so is our capacity.
WILLIAM HAZLITT

Who has self-confidence will lead the rest.
HORACE

The team that won't be beaten, can't be beaten.
FRANK BROYLES

A workout makes you better today than you were yesterday. It strengthens the body, relaxes the mind, and toughens the spirit. When you work out regularly, your problems diminish and your confidence grows.
ANONYMOUS

The only limit to our realization of tomorrow will be our doubts of today.
FRANKLIN D. ROOSEVELT

# Confidence

In order to succeed, we must first believe
we can.
MICHAEL KORDA

Confidence is contagious, as is lack of
confidence.
VINCE LOMBARDI

I don't think we can win every game. Just
the next one.
LOU HOLTZ

Self-trust, we know, is the first secret of
success.
LADY WILDE

Fear is your best friend or your worst
enemy. It's like fire. If you can control it, it can cook
for you; it can heat your house. If you can't control
it, it will burn you every time.
CUS D'AMATO

Confidence is a lot of this game or any
game. If you don't think you can, you won't.
JERRY WEST

I have confidence in my ability. You have to. If you don't, who will?
JOHNNY UNITAS

I'm not out there just to be dancing around. I expect to win every time I tee up.
LEE TREVINO

I am only one, but I am one. I cannot do everything, but I can do something. What I can do, I should do and, with the help of God, I will do!
EVERETT HALE

If one advances confidently in the direction of his dreams, and endeavours to live the life which he has imagined, he will meet with a success unexpected in common hours.
HENRY DAVID THOREAU

Do not attempt to do a thing unless you are sure of yourself; but do not relinquish it simply because someone else is not sure of you.
STEWART E. WHITE

# Courage

The greatest test of courage on earth is to beat defeat without losing heart.
ROBERT G. INGERSOLL

He who is not courageous enough to take risks will accomplish nothing in life.
MUHAMMAD ALI

You must do the thing you think you cannot do.
ELEANOR ROOSEVELT

A ship in a harbour is safe, but that is not what ships are built for.
ANONYMOUS

A hero is no braver than an ordinary man, but he is brave five minutes longer.
RALPH WALDO EMERSON

The most effective way to ensure the value of the future is to confront the present courageously and constructively.
ROLLO MAY

None but a coward dares to boast that he has never known fear.
FERDINAND FOCH

Don't be afraid to take a big step. You can't cross a chasm in two small jumps.
ANONYMOUS

That man is not truly brave who is afraid either to seem to be, or to be, when it suits him, a coward.
EDGAR ALLAN POE

He who fears he shall suffer, already suffers what he fears.
MICHEL EYQUEM DE MONTAIGNE

To see what is right and not do it is want of courage.
CONFUCIUS

We should never let our fears hold us back from pursuing our hopes.
JOHN F. KENNEDY

# Courage

Courage is the thing. All goes if courage goes.
Sir J. M. Barrie

Some have been thought brave because they were afraid to run away.
Thomas Fuller

It was a high counsel that I once heard given to a young person, 'Always do what you are afraid to do.'
Ralph Waldo Emerson

It is better to die on your feet than to live on your knees.
Dolores Ibárruri

Behold the turtle – he only makes progress when he sticks his neck out.
Anonymous

When you have faults, do not fear to abandon them.
Confucius

Courage – or putting it more accurately, lack of fear – is a result of discipline. By an act of will, a man refuses to think of the reasons for fear, and so concentrates entirely on winning the battle.
RICHARD NIXON

Keep your fears to yourself, but share your courage.
ROBERT LOUIS STEVENSON

The impossible can only be overborne by the unprecedented.
SIR IAN HAMILTON

If a man never fails, it may be because he never tries.
ANONYMOUS

Courage, that is the temporary domination of will over instinct, brings about victory.
ARDANT DU PICQ

Bravery is being the only one who knows you're afraid.
FRANKLIN P. JONES

# Courage

Life only demands from you the strength you possess. Only one feat is possible – not to have run away.
DAG HAMMARSKJOLD

I believe that anyone can conquer fear by doing the things he fears to do, provided he keeps doing them until he gets a record of successful experiences behind him.
ELEANOR ROOSEVELT

You can't steal second base and keep your foot on first.
ANONYMOUS

A timid person is frightened before a danger, a coward during the time, and a courageous person afterwards.
JEAN PAUL RICHTER

Courage is grace under pressure.
WINSTON CHURCHILL

Fortune sides with him who dares.
VIRGIL

Great crises produce great men and great deeds of courage.
JOHN F. KENNEDY

We're all in this alone.
LILY TOMLIN

Make up your mind to act decidedly and take the consequences. No good is ever done in this world by hesitation.
THOMAS HENRY HUXLEY

Courage is very important. Like a muscle, it is strengthened by use.
RUTH GORDON

You have to have courage to make a decision and stick with it knowing people are going to criticize you no matter what you do.
ANONYMOUS

Everyone has talent. What is rare is the courage to follow the talent to the dark place where it leads.
ERICA JONG

# *Courage*

It is easy to be brave from a safe distance.

AESOP

Nothing gives a fearful man more courage than another's fear.

UMBERTO ECO

If you never take a chance you will never be defeated – but you will never accomplish anything either.

ANONYMOUS

You take a number of small steps which you believe are right, thinking maybe tomorrow somebody will treat this as a dangerous provocation. And then you wait. If there is no reaction, you take another step – courage is only an accumulation of small steps.

GEORGE KONRAD

The only thing we have to fear is fear itself.

FRANKLIN D. ROOSEVELT

All serious daring starts from within.

EUDORA WELTY

You cannot discover new oceans unless you have the courage to lose sight of the shore.
ANONYMOUS

No one can answer for his courage when he has never been in danger.
FRANÇOIS DE LA ROCHEFOUCAULD

The pressure of adversity does not affect the mind of the brave man.... It is more powerful than external circumstances.
LUCIUS ANNAEUS SENECA

Bravery is the capacity to perform properly even when scared half to death.
OMAR NELSON BRADLEY

What would life be if we had no courage to attempt anything?
VINCENT VAN GOGH

And the trouble is, if you don't risk anything, you risk even more.
ERICA JONG

# Courage

The crime is not to avoid failure. The crime is not to give triumph a chance.
HUW WHELDON

Maturity is the ability to make a decision and stand by it. The immature spend their lives exploring endless possibilities; then they do nothing.
ANONYMOUS

Without justice, courage is weak.
BENJAMIN FRANKLIN

A great part of courage is the courage of having done the thing before.
RALPH WALDO EMERSON

He who fears something gives it power over him.
MOORISH PROVERB

The only thing that stands between a man and what he wants from life is often merely the will to try it and faith to believe that it is possible.
RICHARD DEVOS

Don't be afraid to go out on a limb—that is where the fruit is.
ANONYMOUS

Just as courage imperils life, fear protects it.
LEONARDO DA VINCI

Courage is the first of human qualities because it is the quality which guarantees all others.
WINSTON CHURCHILL

The will to do, the tenacity to overcome all obstacles and finish the course is rooted in courage.
J. EDGAR HOOVER

Nothing ventured, nothing gained.
WILLIAM SHAKESPEARE

Courage consists not in blindly overlooking danger, but in seeing it and conquering it.
ANONYMOUS

To win you have to risk losing.
JEAN-CLAUDE KILLY

# Courage

No one knows what it is that he can do till he tries.
PUBLILIUS SYRUS

Success is never final and failure is never fatal. It is courage that counts.
WINSTON CHURCHILL

He who loses wealth loses much; he who loses a friend loses more; he who loses courage loses all.
MIGUEL DE CERVANTES

Take into account that great love and great achievements involve great risk.
ANONYMOUS

Courage is resistance to fear, mastery of fear—not absence of fear.
MARK TWAIN

I swing big, with everything I've got. I hit big or I miss big. I like to live as big as I can.
BABE RUTH

Life shrinks and expands in proportion to one's courage.
ANAIS NIN

Risk more than others think is safe.
ANONYMOUS

Fortune favours the brave.
TERENCE

It is not because things are difficult that we do not dare; it is because we do not dare that things are difficult.
LUCIUS ANNAEUS SENECA

Life was meant to be lived and curiosity must be kept alive. One must never, for whatever reason, turn his back on life.
ELEANOR ROOSEVELT

There is the risk you cannot afford to take, and there is the risk you cannot afford not to take.
PETER F. DRUCKER

# Desire

Some men are bigger, faster, stronger, and smarter than others—but not a single man has a corner on dreams, desire, or ambition.

DUFFY DAUGHERTY

Desire! That's the one secret of every man's career. Not education. Not being born with hidden talents. Desire.

BOBBY UNSER

We desire most what we ought not to have.

PUBLILIUS SYRUS

A strong passion for any object will ensure success, for the desire of the end will point out the means.

WILLIAM HAZLITT

A champion must have the desire for perfection, and the will to punish himself in the process.

ANONYMOUS

Follow your dream.

JOSEPH CAMPBELL

$S$uccess is focusing the full power of all you are on what you have a burning desire to achieve.
WILFERD A. PETERSON

$T$here couldn't be a society of people who didn't dream. They'd be dead in two weeks.
WILLIAM BURROUGHS

$W$e accomplish things by directing our desires, not ignoring them.
JOHN HENRY NEWMAN

$S$trength is not nearly as important as desire. I don't think you can teach anyone desire. I think it's a gift. I don't know why I have it, but I do.
LARRY BIRD

$I$f everyone got what they wanted, there wouldn't be enough to go around.
ANONYMOUS

$T$he future is like heaven – everyone exalts it but no one wants to go there now.
JAMES BALDWIN

# Desire

Man's desires are limited by his perceptions; none can desire what he has not perceiv'd.
WILLIAM BLAKE

Often, the thing we pursue most passionately is but a substitute for the one thing we really want and cannot have.
ERIC HOFFER

You see things that are and say, "Why?" But you dream things that never were and say, "Why not?"
ANONYMOUS

We do not succeed in changing things according to our desire, but gradually our desire changes.
MARCEL PROUST

If one advances confidently in the direction of his dreams, and endeavours to live the life which he has imagined, he will meet with a success unexpected in common hours.
HENRY DAVID THOREAU

The desire of knowledge, like the thirst of riches, increases ever with the acquisition of it.
LAURENCE STERNE

Always keep the heart young and expectations high, and never let your dreams die.
ANONYMOUS

We are less dissatisfied when we lack many things than when we seem to lack but one thing.
ERIC HOFFER

If you really want something, you can figure out how to make it happen.
CHER

The first principle of success is desire— knowing what you want. Desire is the planting of your seed.
ROBERT COLLIER

First deserve, then desire.
PROVERB

# Determination

The heights by great men reached and kept
Were not attained by sudden flight,
But they, while their companions slept,
Were toiling upward in the night.
HENRY WADSWORTH LONGFELLOW

Successful men make up their minds what they want and then go after it with everything in them.
ANONYMOUS

Winners never quit and quitters never win.
VINCE LOMBARDI

The person who succeeds is not the one who holds back, fearing failure, nor the one who never fails, but rather the one who moves on in spite of failure.
ANONYMOUS

Never—never—never—never give up!
WINSTON CHURCHILL

No will to win – no way you'll win!
ANONYMOUS

Some succeed because they are destined to, but most succeed because they are determined to.
ANONYMOUS

Although the world is full of suffering, it is also full of the overcoming of it.
HELEN KELLER

A diamond is a chunk of coal that made good under pressure.
ANONYMOUS

The world breaks everyone and afterward many are strong at the broken places.
ERNEST HEMINGWAY

The guy who gets ahead, is the guy who does more than is necessary—and keeps on doing it.
ANONYMOUS

I learned that the only way you are going to get anywhere in life is to work hard at it. If you do, you'll win—if you don't, you won't.
BRUCE JENNER

# Determination

Success is determined by how determined you are to succeed.
ANONYMOUS

Don't let life discourage you; everyone who got where he is had to begin where he was.
RICHARD L. EVANS

In the confrontation between the stream and the rock, the stream always wins—not through strength, but by perseverance.
ANONYMOUS

The price of victory is high: blood, sweat, tears, frustration, and sometimes defeat.
ANONYMOUS

We fought hard. We gave it our best. We did what was right and we made a difference.
GERALDINE A. FERRARO

A successful person is one who went ahead and did the thing the rest of us never quite got around to.
ANONYMOUS

Even the woodpecker owes his success to the fact that he uses his head and keeps pecking away until he finishes the job he starts.
B. C. FORBES

Maturity is perseverance, the ability to sweat out a project or a situation in spite of heavy opposition and discouraging setbacks.
ANONYMOUS

Success doesn't come to you… you go to it.
MARVA COLLINS

To get ahead you usually have to push someone ahead of you. It also helps to be pushed by someone behind you.
ANONYMOUS

If it is meant to be, it is up to me.
SHERRY BASSIN

Success is not a matter of luck or of genius. Success depends on adequate preparation and determination.
ANONYMOUS

# Determination

The key to success is to climb the ladder instead of waiting for the elevator.
ANONYMOUS

People who win many have been counted out several times, but they didn't hear the referee.
H. E. JANSON

Most things are difficult before they are easy. The difference between playing to win and playing not to lose is often the difference between success and mediocrity.
ANONYMOUS

We must either find a way or make one.
HANNIBAL

The great thing in this world is not so much where we are, but in what direction we are moving.
OLIVER WENDELL HOLMES

There's only one method of meeting life's test: Just keep striving and hope for the best.
ANONYMOUS

For about two weeks, every boy who had tried out for the basketball team at my high school knew what day the cut list was going to go up. We knew it was going to be posted in the gym, in the morning. So that morning we all went in there, and the list was up. We stood there and looked for our names. If your name was on the list, you were still on the team. If your name wasn't on the list, you were cut. Mine wasn't on the list.

I looked and looked for my name. I looked at the H's, and the I's, and the J's, and the K's, and I wasn't there, and I went back and started again. But I wasn't there.

I went through that day numb. I sat through my classes. I had to wait until after school to go home. That's when I hurried to my house and closed the door to my room and I cried so hard. It was all I wanted—to play on that team.

MICHAEL JORDAN

Never let up. The more you can win by, the more doubts you put in the other players' minds the next time out.

SAM SNEAD

The door of success opens with a push.

ANONYMOUS

# Discipline

**S**weat plus sacrifice equals success.

**A**lways keep your composure. You can't score from the penalty box; and to win, you have to score.
BOBBY HULL

**I**f you want a place in the sun, you will have to expect some blisters.
ANONYMOUS

**H**e that can have patience can have what he will.
BENJAMIN FRANKLIN

**O**nly those who have the patience to do simple things perfectly will acquire the skill to do difficult things easily.
ANONYMOUS

**W**e forget our faults easily when they are known to ourselves alone.
FRANÇOIS DE LA ROCHEFOUCAULD

There are no secrets to success. Success is doing the things you know you should do.
ANONYMOUS

Do your duty in all things. You cannot do more. You should never wish to do less.
ROBERT E. LEE

It is easier to do a good job than to explain why you did not.
ANONYMOUS

I count him braver who overcomes his desires than him who overcomes his enemies.
ARISTOTLE

The problem is not that people don't know what to do. The problem is they find reasons not to do it until there are no tomorrows.
ANONYMOUS

Only those who have disciplined themselves can exact disciplined performance from others.
MATTHEW B RIDGWAY

# Discipline

Growl all day and you'll be dog tired by night.
ANONYMOUS

Football is like life – it requires perseverance, self-denial, hard work, sacrifice, dedication, and respect for authority.
VINCE LOMBARDI

The hot games are won by those with cool heads.
ANONYMOUS

Few men are born brave; many become so through training and force of discipline.
VEGETIUS

Anything is yours if you are willing to pay the price.
ANONYMOUS

Hard work has made it easy. That is my secret. That is why I win.
NADIA COMANECI

There is a big difference between wanting to and willing to.
ANONYMOUS

The only discipline that lasts is self-discipline.
BUM PHILLIPS

Greatness cannot be achieved without discipline.
ANONYMOUS

Good habits are hard to form but easy to live with. Bad habits are easy to form but hard to live with.
ANONYMOUS

Habit is overcome by habit.
THOMAS A KEMPIS

The reason some men do not succeed is because their wishbone is where their backbone ought to be.
ANONYMOUS

# *Discipline*

The chains of habit are too weak to be felt until they are too strong to be broken.
SAMUEL JOHNSON

A lot of people love their jobs. It's the work they hate.
ANONYMOUS

A man must learn to endure that patiently which he cannot avoid conveniently.
MICHEL EYQUEM DE MONTAIGNE

Hard work never killed anyone—but some people get real sick doing it.
ANONYMOUS

Our patience will achieve more than our force.
EDMUND BURKE

The person who does what he pleases is seldom pleased with what he does.
ANONYMOUS

To be a winner you have to say no to pleasures an athlete cannot afford.
ANONYMOUS

Patience is bitter, but its fruits are sweet.
JEAN JACQUES ROUSSEAU

Remember that winners do what losers don't want to.
ANONYMOUS

I've always felt it was not up to anyone else to make me give my best.
HAKEEM OLAJUWON

Everything comes to those who wait—if they work while they wait.
ANONYMOUS

# Effort

I never did anything worth doing by accident, nor did any of my inventions come by accident. They came by work.
THOMAS ALVA EDISON

Winning isn't everything, but making the effort to win is.
VINCE LOMBARDI

Try to live on the principle, 'Nothing attempted, nothing gained,' and if you fail, you are going to fail while trying to succeed.
ANONYMOUS

I see no virtue where I smell no sweat.
FRANCIS QUARLES

Nothing good comes in life or athletics unless a lot of hard work has preceded the effort. Only temporary success is achieved by taking short cuts.
ROGER STAUBACH

I had rather wear out than rust out.
GEORGE WHITEFIELD

$N$o amount of pay ever made a good soldier, a good teacher, a good artist, or a good workman.
JOHN RUSKIN

$Y$ou add try and umph… see what you come up with.
ANONYMOUS

$T$he manly part is to do with might and main what you can do.
RALPH WALDO EMERSON

$A$lways begin somewhere. You cannot build a reputation on what you intend to do.
ANONYMOUS

$I$n all things do your best…. The man who has done his best has done everything. The man who has done less than his best has done nothing.
CHARLES M. SCHWAB

$I$ would rather be a brilliant memory than a curiosity.
EMMA EAMES

# *Effort*

The best angle from which to approach any problem is the *try*-angle.
ANONYMOUS

There is no failure except in no longer trying.
ELBERT HUBBARD

Doing the best you are capable of is victory; doing less is defeat.
ANONYMOUS

I firmly believe that any man's finest hour, his greatest fulfillment to all he holds dear, is the moment when he has worked his heart out in a good cause and lies exhausted on the field of battle victorious.
VINCE LOMBARDI

Hustle! You can't survive without it.
ANONYMOUS

God doesn't require us to succeed; he only requires that you try.
MOTHER TERESA

The difference between good and great is a little extra effort.
ANONYMOUS

Nothing is so certain as that the evils of idleness can be shaken off by hard work.
LUCIUS ANNAEUS SENECA

Hard work beats talent, unless talent works.
ANONYMOUS

To try to be better is to be better.
CHARLOTTE CUSHMAN

Even a mosquito doesn't get a slap on the back until he starts to work.
ANONYMOUS

To youth I have but three words of counsel – work, work, work.
OTTO VON BISMARCK

In the end, the only people who fail are those who do not try.
ANONYMOUS

# *Effort*

**W**hatever muscles I have are the product of my own hard work—nothing else.
EVELYN ASHFORD

**I**t takes work to take over.
ED SHURNA

**Y**our rewards in life are always in direct proportion to your contribution.
ANONYMOUS

**T**he important thing in the Olympic Games is not to win but to take part; the important thing in life is not the triumph but the struggle. The essential thing is not to have conquered but to have fought well.
BARON PIERRE DE COUBERTIN

**N**ever discourage anyone who makes progress, no matter how slow.
PLATO

**W**hat really counts is not the number of hours you put in, but how much you put in the hours.
ANONYMOUS

If you aspire to the highest place, it is no disgrace to stop at the second, or even third, place.
MARCUS TULLIUS CICERO

If better is ever possible, good is not good enough.
ANONYMOUS

I think the harder you work, the more luck you have.
R. DAVID THOMAS

Always do your best. What you plant now, you will harvest later.
OG MANDINO

Take the initiative and work hard. Ask questions, look for opportunity, but don't wait for success to come to you.
ANONYMOUS

I'm like a duck: calm above water, but paddling like hell underneath.
FRED SHERO

# Effort

Life does not require that we become the biggest or the best, only that we try.
ANONYMOUS

There are very few things in this world worth having that can be had cheaply.
FRANCIS G. PEABODY

There is no substitute for work. It is the price of success.
EARL BLAIK

Don't judge those who try and fail. Judge only those who fail to try.
ANONYMOUS

The human body is the only machine that breaks down when not used. Moreover, it is the only mechanism that functions better and more healthily the more it is put to use.
DR. T. K. CURETON

The harder you work, the harder it is to surrender.
VINCE LOMBARDI

I do the best I know how, the very best I can; and I mean to keep on doing it to the end.
ABRAHAM LINCOLN

Do it like it's your last chance.
ANONYMOUS

Success is peace of mind in knowing that you did your best to become the best that you are capable of becoming.
JOHN WOODEN

There are no gains without pains.
ADLAI STEVENSON

Fatigue makes cowards of us all.
VINCE LOMBARDI

You prove your worth with your actions, not with your mouth.
PAT RILEY

Sweat is the ornament of virtue's face.
HESIOD

# Effort

The amount of success you are able to achieve through wisdom will be in direct proportion to the effort expended in acquiring it.
ANONYMOUS

No man fails who does his best.
ORISON SWETT MARDEN

The dictionary is the only place success comes before work. Hard work is the price we must all pay for success.
VINCE LOMBARDI

Nobody who ever gave his best regretted it.
GEORGE HALAS

No one can predict to what heights you can soar. Even you will not know until you spread your wings.
ANONYMOUS

It is said that good things come to those who wait. I believe that good things come to those who work.
WILT CHAMBERLAIN

It doesn't take any ability to hustle.

BILLY MARTIN


Those who profit most are those who give the most.

ANONYMOUS


Push yourself again and again. Don't give an inch until the final buzzer.

LARRY BIRD


If one has not given everything, one has given nothing.

GEORGES GUYNEMER


What we hope ever to do with ease, we must learn first to do with diligence.

SAMUEL JOHNSON


You are never given a wish without also being given the power to make it come true. You may have to work for it, however.

RICHARD BACH

# Enthusiasm

Nothing great was ever achieved without enthusiasm.
RALPH WALDO EMERSON

If you aren't fired with enthusiasm, you will be fired with enthusiasm.
VINCE LOMBARDI

Zeal is like fire – it needs both feeding and watching.
PROVERB

Winners forget they are in a race. They just love to run.
ANONYMOUS

Enjoyment is *not* a goal; it is a feeling that accompanies important ongoing activity.
PAUL GOODMAN

When you are making a success of something, it's not work. It's a way of life. You enjoy yourself because you are making your contribution to the world.
ANDY GRANATELLI

I can feel the wind go by when I run. It feels good. It feels fast.
EVELYN ASHFORD

I studied the lives of great men and women, and I found that the men and women who got to the top were those who did the jobs they had in hand, with everything they had of energy and enthusiasm and hard work.
HARRY S. TRUMAN

As long as I can focus on enjoying what I'm doing, having fun, I know I'll play well.
STEFFI GRAF

Success is not the result of spontaneous combustion. You must set yourself on fire first.
REGGIE LEACH

Conscience and reason will have the last word. Passion will have the last deed.
ANONYMOUS

Sports is the toy department of human life.
HOWARD COSELL

# Enthusiasm

I'd rather swing a bat than do anything else in the world.
TED WILLIAMS

Work and play are words used to describe the same thing under differing conditions.
MARK TWAIN

Enthusiasm is like a coat of fresh paint; it covers up a lot of rough spots.
ANONYMOUS

You've got to love what you're doing. If you love it, you can overcome any handicap or the soreness or all the aches and pains, and continue to play for a long, long time.
GORDIE HOWE

Don't drop out, drop in. Don't cop out, compete. Don't exit, excel.
PIERRE TRUDEAU

Enthusiasm is the yeast that raises the dough.
ANONYMOUS

I think I'll work all my life. When you're having fun, why stop having fun?
HELEN THOMAS

The most important thing is to love your sport. Never do it to please someone else. It has to be yours.
PEGGY FLEMING

The reason I love conducting is that I love the people for whom we play… it's the most potent love affair you can have in your life.
LEONARD BERNSTEIN

Nothing great in the world has ever been accomplished without passion.
HEGEL

There is a real magic in enthusiasm. It spells the difference between mediocrity and accomplishment.
NORMAN VINCENT PEALE

Charisma is the transference of enthusiasm.
RALPH ARCHBOLD

# Enthusiasm

Enthusiasm moves the world.
ARTHUR JAMES BALFOUR

Good science consists largely of play disguised as serious work.
EDMUND WILSON

Enthusiasm is the greatest asset in the world. It beats money, power, and influence.
HENRY CHESTER

Enthusiasm is a vital element toward the individual success of every man or woman.
CONRAD HILTON

Without enthusiasm you are doomed to a life of mediocrity, but with it you can accomplish miracles.
OG MANDINO

No battle of any importance can be won without enthusiasm.
JOHN LORD O'BRIAN

Enthusiasm… the sustaining power of all great action.
SAMUEL SMILES

Catch on fire with enthusiasm, and people will come for miles to watch you burn.
JOHN WESLEY

Every production of genius must be the production of enthusiasm.
BENJAMIN DISRAELI

One man has enthusiasm for 30 minutes, another for 30 days, but it is the man who has it for 30 years who makes a success of his life.
EDWARD B. BUTLER

# Excellence

In the pursuit of excellence, there is no finish line.
ROBERT H. FORMAN

Nobody can achieve perfection; but in the pursuit of perfection, one can obtain excellence.
VINCE LOMBARDI

People are not excellent because they achieve great things; they achieve great things because they choose to be excellent.
ANONYMOUS

One machine can do the work of fifty ordinary men. No machine can do the work of one extraordinary man.
ELBERT HUBBARD

Man is the only creature that strives to surpass himself, and yearns for the impossible.
ERIC HOFFER

True greatness consists in being great in little things.
ANONYMOUS

With regard to excellence, it is not enough to know, but we must try to have and use it.
ARISTOTLE

The same man cannot well be skilled in everything; each has his special excellence.
EURIPEDES

If it's worth doing at all, it's worth doing well.
ANONYMOUS

No one ever got far by working a 40-hour week. Most of the notable people I know are trying to manage a 40-hour day.
CHANNING POLLOCK

Unless you are willing to drench yourself in your work beyond the capacity of the average man, you are just not cut out for positions at the top.
J. C. PENNEY

He wishes not to seem, but to be, the best.
AESCHYLUS

# Excellence

**W**inning isn't everything, but it beats anything that comes in second.
PAUL 'BEAR' BRYANT

**A** winner says, "I'm good, but I ought to be better." A loser says, "I'm not as bad as lots of other people."
ANONYMOUS

**Y**ou could be the world's best garbage man, the world's best model; it doesn't matter what you do if you're the best.
MUHAMMAD ALI

**N**ot doing more than the average is what keeps the average down.
WILLIAM M. WINANS

**E**xcellence can be attained if you care more than others think is wise.
ANONYMOUS

**I**t isn't hard to be good from time to time in sports. What's tough is being good every day.
WILLIE MAYS

The only sin is mediocrity.

MARTHA GRAHAM

The secret of joy in work is contained in one word—excellence. To know how to do something well is to enjoy it.

PEARL S. BUCK

Strive for excellence, not perfection.

ANONYMOUS

The quality of a person's life is in direct proportion to their commitment to excellence.

VINCE LOMBARDI

Do more than you have to do, more than your share, and do it as well as you can.

ANONYMOUS

I want to do more than anyone else could, using opportunities to do more than just survive. I want to be better than I was the day before, every single day that I'm alive.

DARYL BUSH

# Excellence

Good, better, best. Never let it rest, until your good is better and your better is best.
ANONYMOUS

It takes a long time to bring excellence to maturity.
PUBLILIUS SYRUS

We are what we repeatedly do.... Excellence, then, is not an act but a habit.
ARISTOTLE

Hold yourself responsible for a higher standard than anyone expects from you.
ANONYMOUS

A good man isn't good for everything.
JOHN W. GARDNER

I know it sounds selfish, wanting to do something no one else has done. But that's what you're out here for... to separate yourself from everyone else.
JACK NICKLAUS

Excellence is the exceptional drive to exceed expectations.
ANONYMOUS

If you're going to do it, do it right.
LEE IOCACCA

I will demand a commitment to excellence and to victory and that is what life is all about.
VINCE LOMBARDI

All the rings, all the colour, all the money, and all the display linger in the memory only a short time and are soon forgotten. But the will to win, the will to excel, these are things that endure and are so much more important than any of the events that occasion them.
ANONYMOUS

You have to improve your club, even if it means letting your grown brother go.
TIM MCCARVER

It is wrong if it is almost right.
ANONYMOUS

# Excellence

Next year is not about winning another championship, or having one more ring, or developing bigger reputations. It's about leaving footprints.

PAT RILEY

If you aren't going all the way, why go at all?

JOE NAMATH

Success is perishable and often outside our control. In contrast, excellence is something that's lasting, dependable, and largely within a person's control.

JOE PATERNO

The reward of a task well done is in being called to do a bigger one.

ANONYMOUS

I put the most pressure on myself because of my ambition to be the best basketball player ever. What happens around me can't put any more pressure on me than that.

JULIUS ERVING

I don't ask our athletes how many of them want to win. The question I ask is can you live with losing, can you live with failure, can you live with mediocrity?
LOU HOLTZ

Welcome the task that makes you go beyond yourself.
FRANK MCGEE

If you think you are good, then why not be better. If you think you are better, then be the best.
ANONYMOUS

All things excellent are difficult, as they are rare.
BARUCH SPINOZA

The greatest thing a man can do in this world is to make the most possible out of the stuff that has been given him.
ORISON SWETT MARDEN

A man is judged by what he finishes, not by what he starts.
ANONYMOUS

# Focus

You always have to focus in life on what you want to achieve.
MICHAEL JORDAN

Nothing can add more power to your life than concentrating all of your energies on a limited set of targets.
NIDO QUBEIN

Yesterday is not ours to recover, but tomorrow is ours to win or lose.
LYNDON BAINES JOHNSON

Some people dream of worthy accomplishments, while others stay awake and do them.
ANONYMOUS

One thought driven home is better than three left on base.
JAMES LITER

You can destroy your now by worrying about tomorrow.
JANIS JOPLIN

A parrot talks much but flies little.
ANONYMOUS

Do not look back. And do not dream about the future, either. It will neither give you back the past, nor satisfy your other daydreams. Your duty, your reward – your destiny – are here and now.
DAG HAMMARSKJÖLD

The big print giveth and the fine print taketh away.
J. FULTON SHEEN

The only game we want to win is the next one.
ANONYMOUS

Two things a man should never be angry at: what he can help, and what he cannot help.
THOMAS FULLER

Focus… is a process of diverting one's scattered forces into one powerful channel.
JAMES ALLEN

# *Focus*

Never put off until tomorrow what you can avoid altogether.

ANONYMOUS

When every physical and mental resource is focused, one's power to solve a problem multiplies tremendously.

NORMAN VINCENT PEALE

Who begins too much accomplishes little.

GERMAN PROVERB

There ain't nothing matters less than what you did yesterday.

PETER DEXTER (Character T.D. Davis), *God's Pocket*

When a man imagines that he has attained perfection, his decline begins.

ANONYMOUS

I don't play golf, I don't go to the movies. I get up at 3 o'clock every morning, and I haven't missed a day in 10 years. I've got tunnel vision about my work. I train horses.

D. WAYNE LUKAS

Executives are like joggers. If you stop a jogger, he goes on running on the spot. If you drag an executive away from his business, he goes on running on the spot, pawing the ground, talking business. He never stops hurtling onwards, making decisions and executing them.
JEAN BAUDRILLARD


Learn to focus on one thing and finish it.
ANONYMOUS


One never notices what has been done; one can only see what remains to be done.
MARIE CURIE


The minute you start talking about what you are going to do if you lose, you have lost.
GEORGE SCHULTZ


When success turns an athlete's head, he faces failure.
ANONYMOUS


You get out in front—you stay out in front.
A. J. FOYT

# *Focus*

**S**uccess demands singleness of purpose.
ANONYMOUS

**I**'m trying to do the best I can. I'm not concerned about tomorrow, but with what goes on today.
MARK SPITZ

**Y**ou must be single minded. Drive for the one thing on which you have decided.
GEORGE S. PATTON

**T**he great challenge of life is to decide what's important and to disregard everything else.
ANONYMOUS

**I** believe when you are in any contest, you should work as though there is, to the very last minute, a chance to lose.
DWIGHT D. EISENHOWER

**T**here is no point at which you can say, "Well, I'm successful now. I might as well take a nap."
CARRIE FISHER

Forget about style; worry about results.

BOBBY ORR

Those who attain to any excellence commonly spend life in some single pursuit, for excellence is not often gained upon easier terms.

SAMUEL JOHNSON

Give whatever you are doing and whoever you are with the gift of your attention.

JIM ROHN

I'm trying not to look too far ahead. All I'm thinking is one shot at a time, one hole at a time, and that's what I want to keep doing.

MICHELLE MCGANN

# Goals

All my life I wanted to be somebody. Now I see that I should have been more specific.
JANE WAGNER

Goals are dreams with deadlines.
DIANA SCHARF HUNT

Be aware that the only ceiling life has is the one you give it.
ANONYMOUS

When I am working on a problem, I never think about beauty. I think only of how to solve the problem. But when I have finished, if the solution is not beautiful, I know it is wrong.
BUCKMINSTER FULLER

We see obstacles when we take our eyes off our goals.
ANONYMOUS

Acting without thinking is like shooting without aiming.
B. C. FORBES

$V$isualize yourself as the player you want to be.
ANONYMOUS

$I$f a man takes no thought about what is distant, he will find sorrow near at hand.
CONFUCIUS

$I$ believe in mountains; they are a practical reminder of how high I must reach.
ANONYMOUS

$A$ good plan executed right now is far better than a perfect plan executed next week.
GEORGE S. PATTON

$I$f you don't set goals for yourself, you are doomed to work to achieve the goals of someone else.
ANONYMOUS

$A$ man's worth is no greater than the worth of his ambitions.
MARCUS AURELIUS ANTONINUS

# Goals

To understand the present you must know the past. Knowing the past helps you plan the future.
ANONYMOUS

All ambitions are lawful except those which climb upward on the miseries or credulities of mankind.
JOSEPH CONRAD

Create mental pictures of your goals, then work to make those pictures become realities.
ANONYMOUS

Set your goal higher than you can reach – then reach it.
GLENN STEWARD

Above all be of single aim; have a legitimate and useful purpose, and devote yourself unreservedly to it.
ANONYMOUS

Planning is bringing the future into the present so that you can do something about it now.
ALAN LAKEIN

Most people fail not because they aim too high—but because they aim at nothing.
ANONYMOUS

If you would hit the mark, you must aim a little above it;
Every arrow that flies feels the attraction of earth.
HENRY WADSWORTH LONGFELLOW

Before you can score, you must have a goal.
ANONYMOUS

Who shoots at the midday sun, though he be sure he shall never hit the mark, yet as sure he is he shall shoot higher than who aims but at a bush.
SIR PHILIP SIDNEY

Your life can't go according to plan if you have no plan.
ANONYMOUS

A journey of a thousand miles must begin with a single step.
CHINESE PROVERB

# Goals

The trouble with not having a goal is that you can spend your life running up and down the field and never score.
ANONYMOUS

Realize what you really want. It stops you from chasing butterflies and puts you to work digging gold.
WILLIAM MOULTON MARSTON

The trouble with the future is that it usually arrives before we are ready for it.
ANONYMOUS

Winning isn't everything—but wanting to win is.
ARNOLD PALMER

Set a goal – then get rid of those things in your life which keep you from attaining that goal.
ANONYMOUS

Whatever your goal in life, be proud of every day that you are able to work in that direction.
CHRIS EVERT

People who enjoy success have a plan to keep on succeeding.

ANONYMOUS

In the long run, people hit only what they aim at. Therefore, they had better aim at something high.

HENRY DAVID THOREAU

If you don't know where you are going, how can you expect to get there?

BASIL WALSH

He who aims at nothing hits it with remarkable success.

ANONYMOUS

The direction of the mind is more important than its progress.

JOSEPH JOUBERT

# Happiness

Happiness is having a scratch for every itch.
Ogden Nash

The more difficult a victory, the greater the happiness in winning.
Pele

We are more interested in making others believe we are happy than in trying to be happy ourselves.
François de la Rochefoucauld

Enjoy the little things, for one day you may look back and realize they were the big things.
Robert Brault

Contentment consists not in great wealth, but in few wants.
Anonymous

Pleasure is very seldom found where it is sought; our brightest blazes of gladness are commonly kindled by unexpected sparks.
Samuel Johnson

Every possession and every happiness is but lent by chance for an uncertain time, and may therefore be demanded back the next hour.
ARTHUR SCHOPENHAUER

Happiness depends upon ourselves.
ARISTOTLE

The happy man is not he who seems thus to others, but who seems thus to himself.
PUBLILIUS SYRUS

Those who bring sunshine to the lives of others cannot keep it from themselves.
JAMES MATHEW BARRIE

Happiness is a very small desk and a very big wastebasket.
ROBERT ORBEN

Happiness is like coke – something you get as a by-product in the process of making something else.
ALDOUS HUXLEY

# Happiness

What's a man's first duty? The answer's brief: To be himself.
HENRIK IBSEN

There is no duty we so much underrate as the duty of being happy.
ROBERT LOUIS STEVENSON

Variety is the soul of pleasure.
APHRA BEHN

The only happy people I know are the ones who are working well at something they consider important.
ABRAHAM MASLOW

Happiness is loving what you do, even if you don't do it well.
GEORGE BURNS

When one door of happiness closes, another opens; but often we look so long at the closed door that we do not see the one which has been opened for us.
HELEN KELLER

Most men pursue pleasure with such breathless haste that they hurry past it.
SØREN KIERKEGAARD

The purpose of life is the expansion of happiness.
MAHARISHI MAHESH YOGI

Happiness lies not in the mere possession of money; it lies in the joy of achievement, in the thrill of creative effort. The joy and moral stimulation of work no longer must be forgotten in the mad chase after evanescent profits.
FRANKLIN D. ROOSEVELT

I can live for two months on a good compliment.
MARK TWAIN

# Intelligence

Football is a game played with the arms, legs, and shoulders—but mostly from the neck up.
KNUTE ROCKNE

Thinking is the hardest work there is, which is the probable reason why so few engage in it.
HENRY FORD

Everything worth thinking has already been thought; our concern must only be to try to think it through again.
JOHANN WOLFGANG VON GOETHE

Nothing is fool-proof to a sufficiently talented fool.
ANONYMOUS

He that knows least commonly presumes most.
THOMAS FULLER

Far more crucial than what we know or do not know is what we do not want to know.
ERIC HOFFER

Share your knowledge. It's a way to achieve immortality.
ANONYMOUS

Where large sums of money are concerned, it is advisable to trust nobody.
AGATHA CHRISTIE

There is no trusting appearances.
RICHARD BRINSLEY SHERIDAN

How come people who know the least know it the loudest.
ANONYMOUS

Thinking is seeing.
HONORÉ DE BALZAC

Not to know is bad; not to wish to know is worse.
NIGERIAN PROVERB

Activity is the only road to knowledge.
GEORGE BERNARD SHAW

# Intelligence

Light travels faster than sound. That's why people appear bright until you hear them speak.
ANONYMOUS

There is no knowledge that is not power.
RALPH WALDO EMERSON

What you don't know would make a great book.
SYDNEY SMITH

The difference between genius and stupidity is that genius has its limits.
ANONYMOUS

I not only use all the brains I have, but all I can borrow.
WOODROW WILSON

The bold are helpless without cleverness.
EURIPEDES

A feeble mind weakens the body.
JEAN JACQUES ROUSSEAU

Some drink at the fountain of knowledge, others just gargle.
ANONYMOUS

Wealth is the product of man's ability to think.
AYN RAND

What you're thinking, what shape your mind is in, is what makes the biggest difference of all.
WILLIE MAYS

Everybody is ignorant, only on different subjects.
WILL ROGERS

The Lord gave us two ends; one for thinking, one for sitting. Heads you win, tails you lose.
ANONYMOUS

It is better to be approximately right than precisely wrong.
WARREN BUFFETT

# Intelligence

**L**ittle things affect little minds.
BENJAMIN DISRAELI

**T**he key to any game is to use your strengths and hide your weaknesses.
PAUL WESTPHAL

**N**ever attribute to malice that which is explained by stupidity.
ANONYMOUS

**I** think; therefore I am.
RENÉ DESCARTES

**W**here all think alike, no one thinks very much.
WALTER LIPPMANN

**B**etter know nothing than half-know many things.
FRIEDRICH WILHELM NIETZSCHE

**Y**ou play a game with the head and heart.
ANONYMOUS

Intelligence is defined as the ability to adjust.
ANONYMOUS

Nothing can be loved or hated unless it is first known.
LEONARDO DA VINCI

Intelligence is content to point out the road but never drives us along it.
ALEXIS CARREL

To do what others cannot do is talent. To do what talent cannot do is genius.
WILL HENRY

Live intelligently in the present to prepare for the future.
ANONYMOUS

It is not enough to have a good mind. The main thing is to use it well.
RENÉ DESCARTES

# Leadership

To be a leader, you have to make people want to follow you, and nobody wants to follow someone who doesn't know where he's going.
JOE NAMATH

Leadership is the knack of getting somebody to do something you want done because he wants to do it.
DWIGHT D. EISENHOWER

Learn to obey before you command.
SOLON

Man for man, one division is as good as another. They vary only in the skill and leadership of their commanders.
OMAR NELSON BRADLEY

Diplomacy is the art of letting someone else have your way.
ANONYMOUS

Do not go where the path may lead; go instead where there is no path and leave a trail.
RALPH WALDO EMERSON

You can delegate authority, but you can never delegate responsibility for delegating a task to someone else. If you picked the right man, fine, but if you picked the wrong man, the responsibility is yours – not his.
RICHARD E. KRAFVE

He that would govern others, first should be the master of himself.
PHILIP MASSINGER

Encouragement from a good coach can turn an athlete's life around.
ANONYMOUS

It is always easy to obey, if one dreams of being in command.
JEAN-PAUL SARTRE

And when we think we lead, we are most led.
LORD BYRON

Leadership is action, not position.
DONALD H. MCGANNON

# Leadership

**D**eliberation is the work of many men. Action, of one alone.
CHARLES DE GAULLE

**I**f you set up an atmosphere of communication and trust, it becomes a tradition. Older team members will establish your credibility with newer ones. Even if they don't like everything about you, they'll still say, "He's trustworthy, committed to us as a team."
MIKE KRZYZEWSKI

**W**e can often do more for other men by correcting our own faults than by trying to correct theirs.
ANONYMOUS

**A** good leader takes a little more than his share of blame; a little less than his share of credit.
ARNOLD H. GLASGOW

**L**eadership, if the word has any meaning at all, is a characteristic which inheres in individuals who have energy, faith, and ability in unusual degree.
HENRY M. WRISTON

The strength of the group is in the strength of the leader.
VINCE LOMBARDI

A leader is a man who has the ability to get people to do what they don't want to do, and like it.
HARRY S. TRUMAN

To listen well is as powerful a means of influence as to talk well.
ANONYMOUS

Success comes when leaders lead instead of pushing.
S. L. A. MARSHALL

To do great things is difficult; but to command great things is more difficult.
FRIEDRICH WILHELM NIETZSCHE

Only by full use of your imagination and your initiative will you ever know your own capabilities as a leader. You will never know your capacity until you stretch yourself, or are stretched beyond what you think you can do or should do.
ARTHUR G. TRUDEAU

# Leadership

People don't care about how much you know until they know how much you care.
ANONYMOUS

I cannot trust a man to control others who cannot control himself.
ROBERT E. LEE

If it doesn't work, I'll take the blame. You need that courage to be a good coach.
JOHN MCKAY

The superior man is firm in the right way, and not merely firm.
CONFUCIUS

Leaders have two important characteristics: first, they are going somewhere; second, they are able to persuade other people to go with them.
ANONYMOUS

For people are only too glad to obey the man who they believe takes wiser thoughts for their interests than they themselves do.
XENOPHON

First find the man in yourself if you will inspire manliness in others.
AMOS BRONSON ALCOTT


God grant that men of principle shall be our principal men.
THOMAS JEFFERSON


A person cannot teach what he does not know or lead where he does not go.
ANONYMOUS


Treat people as if they were what they ought to be and you help them to become what they are capable of being.
JOHANN WOLFGANG VON GOETHE


Nothing is more difficult, and therefore more precious, than to be able to decide.
NAPOLEON BONAPARTE


To get people to do what they don't want to do in order to achieve what they want to achieve. That is what coaching is all about.
TOM LANDRY

**B**eing ambitious is the best way, by far, for leaders to show their talents.
ANONYMOUS

**A**nyone can hold the helm when the sea is calm.
PUBLILIUS SYRUS

**I** believe some of us must assume leadership. I believe young people thirst to be led to better themselves. Life is hard and success is survival. Leaders inspire us. Leaders show us the way.
FRANK LEAHY

**H**e who seizes the right moment, is the right man.
JOHANN WOLFGANG VON GOETHE

**A** leader has been defined as one who knows the way, goes the way, and shows the way.
ANONYMOUS

**P**eople are human. If you're going to criticize them, compliment them first.
BUM PHILLIPS

Great leaders were first great followers.
ANONYMOUS

He has the right to criticize, who has the heart to help.
ABRAHAM LINCOLN

It's important that people know what you stand for – and what you won't stand for.
MARY WALDRIP

The speed of the leader determines the rate of the pack.
ANONYMOUS

The person always doing his or her best becomes a natural leader, just by example.
JOE DIMAGGIO

Keep away from people who try to belittle your ambitions. Small people always do that, but the really great make you feel that you, too, can become great.
MARK TWAIN

# Leadership

Leaders are like eagles. They don't flock—you find them one at a time.
ANONYMOUS

You don't become a leader because you say you are. It's much more what you do than what you say.
SPARKY ANDERSON

A successful leader has to be innovative. If you are not one step ahead of the crowd, you soon will be a step behind everyone else.
TOM LANDRY

What we want in our business executive is somebody who demands the absolute best in everything, somebody who is never satisfied, somebody who, if he had been in charge of decorating the Sistine Chapel, would have said, "This is a good fresco, Michelangelo, but I want a better fresco, and I want it by tomorrow morning."
DAVE BARRY

Real leaders are ordinary people with extraordinary determination.
ANONYMOUS

Every soldier has a wish to be a general.
RUSSIAN PROVERB

That cause is strong that has… but one strong man behind it.
JAMES RUSSELL LOWELL

You cannot manage men into battle. You manage things, you lead people.
MURRAY HOPPER

No man is fit to command another that cannot command himself.
WILLIAM PENN

Be a leader. Remember the lead sled dog is the only one with a decent view.
ANONYMOUS

The players don't want to see me rushing around and screaming. They want to believe I know what I am doing.
TOM LANDRY

# Leadership

Deep down, your players must know you care about them. This is the most important thing. I could never get away with what I do if the players felt I didn't care. They know, in the long run, I'm in their corner.

BO SCHEMBECHLER

After victory, beware of too much good staying in your hand. It will fast corrupt and warm worms.

RALPH WALDO EMERSON

Be decisive, even if it means you'll sometimes be wrong.

ANONYMOUS

Leadership is getting players to believe in you. If you tell a teammate you're ready to play as tough as you're able to, you'd better go out there and do it. Players will see right through a phony. And they can tell when you're not giving it all you've got. Leadership is diving for a loose ball, getting the crowd involved, getting other players involved. It's being able to take it as well as dish it out. That's the only way you're going to get respect from the players.

LARRY BIRD

The history of the world is full of men who rose to leadership by sheer force of self-confidence, bravery, and tenacity.
MAHATMA GANDHI

The very essence of leadership is that you have to have a vision.
THEODORE HESBURGH

In simplest terms, a leader is one who knows where he wants to go, and gets up, and goes.
JOHN ERKSINE

A real leader faces the music, even when he doesn't like the tune.
ANONYMOUS

A good head and a good heart are always a formidable combination.
NELSON MANDELA

# Learning

Try to learn something about everything and everything about something.
THOMAS HENRY HUXLEY

It is impossible for someone to learn about that which he thinks he knows.
EPICTETUS

Hindsight is an exact science, but nothing is obvious at the outset.
ANONYMOUS

The only things that are going to change you from where you are today to where you are going to be five years from now are the people you meet and the books you read.
LOU HOLTZ

There's only one way of getting rid of one's faults and that is to acquire the habits contradictory to them.
ERNEST DIMNET

There is no reason to repeat bad history.
ELEANOR HOLMES NORTON

A winner shows he is sorry by making up for it; a loser says, "I'm sorry," but does the same thing the next time.
ANONYMOUS

The moment may be temporary, but the memory is forever.
BUD MEYER

The direction in which education starts a man, will determine his future life.
PLATO

Learn the rules so you know how to break them properly.
ANONYMOUS

Time, place, and action may with pain be wrought,
But genius must be born, and never can be taught.
JOHN DRYDEN

They know enough who know how to learn.
HENRY ADAMS

# Learning

The only real mistake is the one from which we learn nothing.
JOHN POWELL

I learned that good judgment comes from experience and that experience grows out of mistakes.
OMAR N. BRADLEY

… that is what learning is. You suddenly understand something you've understood all your life, but in a new way.
DORIS LESSING

Progress comes from the intelligent use of experience.
ANONYMOUS

Just when you think you've graduated from the school of experience, someone thinks up a new course.
MARY WALDRIP

No man's knowledge here can go beyond his experience.
JOHN LOCKE

**K**nowledge advances by steps, and not by leaps.
LORD MACAULAY

**I** never learned anything while I was talking.
ANONYMOUS

**I**f you are going from A to B you do not always necessarily go in a straight line.
MARGARET THATCHER

**A** candle loses nothing by lighting another candle.
FATHER JAMES KELLER

**S**ome people are so busy learning the tricks of the trade, they never learn the trade.
ANONYMOUS

**E**xperience is never limited, and it is never complete; it is an immense sensibility, a kind of huge spider-web of the finest silken threads suspended in the chamber of consciousness, and catching every air-borne particle in its tissue.
HENRY JAMES

# *Learning*

It is better to learn late than never.
ANONYMOUS

Whenever you fall, pick up something.
OSWALD THEODORE AVERY

You cannot train a horse with shouts and expect it to obey a whisper.
DAGABERT D. RUNES

We don't know a millionth of one percent about anything.
THOMAS ALVA EDISON

Any fault recognized is half corrected.
ANONYMOUS

Wise men learn by other men's mistakes, fools by their own.
HENRY GEORGE BOHN

The man who makes no mistakes does not usually make anything.
BISHOP W. C. MAGEE

Constructive criticism is like a soft kick in the rear.
ANONYMOUS

Experience is the name everyone gives to their mistakes.
OSCAR WILDE

Learning without thought is labour lost; thought without learning is perilous.
CONFUCIUS

It is better to know some of the questions than all of the answers.
JAMES THURBER

Nothing is impossible; we merely do not know yet how to do it.
ANONYMOUS

We do not need, and indeed never will have, all the answers before we act.... It is often only through taking action that we can discover some of them.
CHARLOTTE BUNCH

# *Learning*

Learning is not wisdom; information does not guarantee good judgment.
JOHN DEWEY

Do not despise the bottom rungs in the ascent to greatness.
PUBLILIUS SYRUS

Show me a person who has never made a mistake and I'll show you somebody who has never achieved much.
JOAN COLLINS

Experience enables you to recognize a mistake when you make it again.
FRANKLIN P. JONES

Good people are good because they've come to wisdom through failure.
WILLIAM SAROYAN

Experience is not what happens to a man. It is what a man does with what happens to him.
ALDOUS HUXLEY

There is no scrap in scrapbooks.
ANONYMOUS

Learn to see in another's calamity the ills
which you should avoid.
PUBLILIUS SYRUS

Every great mistake has a halfway moment,
a split second when it can be recalled and perhaps
remedied.
PEARL S. BUCK

What we have to learn to do, we have to
learn by doing.
ARISTOTLE

The only job you start out at the top on is
digging a ditch.
WILLIAM ENSLEY

When you make a mistake, there are only
three things you should ever do about it: 1) admit it;
2) learn from it; and 3) don't repeat it.
PAUL 'BEAR' BRYANT

# *Learning*

I hear and I forget. I see and I remember. I do and I understand.
CHINESE PROVERB

A winner says, "There ought to be a better way to do it." A loser says, "That's the way it's always been done here."
ANONYMOUS

A part of control is learning to correct your weaknesses.
BABE RUTH

It's how you deal with failure that determines how you achieve success.
DAVID FEHERTY

Even a mistake may turn out to be the one thing necessary to a worthwhile achievement.
HENRY FORD

He who neglects to drink of the spring of experience is apt to die of thirst in the desert of ignorance.
LING PO

$S$uccess is important, but defeats are valuable.
C. M. JONES

$F$ailure isn't fatal and success isn't final.
ANONYMOUS

$E$very failure teaches a man something if he will learn.
CHARLES DICKENS

$I$f we succeed in giving the love of learning, the learning itself is sure to follow.
SIR JOHN LUBBOCK

$A$ man who makes a mistake and does not correct it is committing another.
CONFUCIUS

$T$he first thing is to know your faults and then take on a systematic plan of correcting them. You know the saying about a chain being only as strong as its weakest link. The same can be said of the chain of skill a man forges.
BABE RUTH

# Learning

May we learn to obey life's rules so that we may be spared its harsh penalties.
ANONYMOUS

A mind stretched by a new idea never returns to its original dimension.
JAMES LINCOLN

It is good to rub and polish your mind against the minds of others.
MICHEL EYQUEM DE MONTAIGNE

When you are through learning, you are through.
ANONYMOUS

The difference between greatness and mediocrity is often how an individual views a mistake.
NELSON BOSWELL

No coach has ever won a game by what he knows; it's what his players have learned.
ALONZO STAGG

A good scare is worth more to a man than good advice.
EDGAR WATSON HOWE

Learn from the mistakes of others – you can never live long enough to make them all yourself.
ANONYMOUS

One thorn of experience is worth a whole wilderness of warning.
JAMES RUSSELL LOWELL

The beautiful thing about learning is nobody can take it away from you.
B. B. KING

To know the road ahead, ask those coming back.
CHINESE PROVERB

Failure is good. It's fertilizer. Everything I've learned about coaching I've learned by making mistakes.
RICK PITINO

# Learning

Most things important to know are difficult to learn.
ANONYMOUS

It's what you know after you know it all that counts.
HARRY S. TRUMAN

The greatest mistake a man can make is to be afraid of making one.
ELBERT HUBBARD

Success is a journey, not a destination.
ANONYMOUS

Failure is the only opportunity to move intelligently to begin again.
HENRY FORD

In this age, which believes that there is a short cut to everything, the greatest lesson to be learned is that the most difficult way is, in the long run, the easiest.
HENRY MILLER

When bad times come, you can let them make you bitter or use them to make you better.
ANONYMOUS

Strange how much you got to know before how little you knew.
DUNCAN STUART

The brighter you are, the more you have to learn.
DON HEROLD

Live as if you were to die tomorrow. Learn as if you were to live forever.
MAHATMA GANDHI

When you lose, don't lose the lesson.
ANONYMOUS

Learn from yesterday, live for today, hope for tomorrow.
ALBERT EINSTEIN

# Motivation

You cannot push anyone up the ladder unless he is willing to climb himself.
ANDREW CARNEGIE

Even if you are on the right track, you'll get run over if you just sit there.
WILL ROGERS

Any criticism I make of anyone on my team, I make because they are not performing to their full potential.
VINCE LOMBARDI

If it weren't for the last minute, nothing would ever get done.
ANONYMOUS

Inspiration could be called inhaling the memory of an act never experienced.
NED ROREM

Despair lames most people, but it wakes others fully up.
WILLIAM JAMES

It's the start that stops most people.
ANONYMOUS

There are many more people trying to meet the right person than to become the right person.
GLORIA STEINEM

There is a saying, 'Well begun is half done' – 'tis a bad one. I would use instead, 'Not begun at all until half done.'
JOHN KEATS

It is an undoubted truth that the less one has to do, the less time one finds to do it in. One yawns, one procrastinates, one can do it when one will, and therefore one seldom does it at all.
LORD CHESTERFIELD

The biggest mistake you can make is to believe that you are working for someone else.
ANONYMOUS

The way to be nothing is to do nothing.
EDGAR WATSON HOWE

# Motivation

You have to take your ego, put it in your back pocket and zip it. If you're waiting for someone to tell you what a good job you're doing, you'll wait a long time.
JIM COVERT

I've learned that you never get rewarded for the things you intended to do.
ANONYMOUS

Too many of us are hung up on what we don't have, can't have, or won't ever have. We spend too much energy being down, when we could use that same energy – if not less of it – doing, or at least trying to do, some of the things we really want to do.
TERRY MCMILLAN

People don't pay much attention when you are second best. I wanted to see what it felt like to be number one.
FLORENCE GRIFFITH JOYNER

Don't wait for your ship to come in; swim out to it.
ANONYMOUS

Deals are my art form. Other people paint beautifully on canvas or write wonderful poetry. I like making deals, preferably big deals. That's how I get my kicks.
DONALD TRUMP

If you don't want to work, you have to earn enough money so you won't have to work.
OGDEN NASH

Every morning in Africa, a gazelle wakes up. It knows that it must run faster than the fastest lion or it will be killed. Every morning a lion wakes up. It knows that it must outrun the slowest gazelle or it will starve to death. It doesn't matter whether you are a lion or a gazelle – when the sun comes up you had better be running.
ANONYMOUS

Life is like a ten-speed bike – most of us have gears we never use.
CHARLES SCHULTZ

We should know mankind better if we were not so anxious to resemble one another.
JOHANN WOLFGANG VON GOETHE

# *Motivation*

The ladder of success doesn't care who climbs it.
FRANK TYGER

Be a self-starter. Create plans and set them in motion. Be a dreamer and a doer.
ANONYMOUS

Man is not the sum of what he has already, but rather the sum of what he does not yet have, of what he could have.
JEAN-PAUL SARTRE

Mankind is divided into three classes: the immovable, the movable, and those who are the movers.
BENJAMIN FRANKLIN

If what you did yesterday still looks big to you, you haven't done much today.
ANONYMOUS

Knowing is not enough – we must apply. Willing is not enough – we must do.
JOHANN WOLFGANG VON GOETHE

We aren't where we want to be, we aren't where we ought to be, but thank goodness we aren't where we used to be.
LOU HOLTZ

I have never heard of someone stumbling on something big while sitting down.
ANONYMOUS

You are today where your thoughts have brought you. You will be tomorrow where your thoughts take you.
JAMES ALLEN

As long as I am improving, I will go on.
MILDRED 'BABE' DIDRIKSON ZAHARIAS

Remember it is better to have little talent and much purpose, than little purpose and much talent.
ANONYMOUS

Hit the ball over the fence and you can take your time going around the bases.
JOHN RAPER

# Motivation

In baseball and in business, there are three types of people. There are those who make it happen, those who watch it happen, and those who wondered what happened.
TOMMY LASORDA

Want to be a champion? Then get to work.
ANONYMOUS

Do more than you're supposed to do and you can have or be or do anything you want.
BILL SANDS

To be a nobody, do nothing.
B. C. FORBES

Remember when you are not practicing, somewhere someone is, and when you meet him, he will win.
ANONYMOUS

What the superior man seeks is in himself; what the small man seeks is in others.
FRANÇOIS DE LA ROCHEFOUCAULD

Seize the day.
HORACE

Ideas will not keep. Something must be done about them.
ANONYMOUS

Anything you can do, or think you can— begin it. Once started, the mind grows heated. Begin the job and the work will be completed.
JOHANN WOLFGANG VON GOETHE

You can't get much done in life if you only work on the days when you feel good.
JERRY WEST

You can stand by and watch the world go by—and it will.
ANONYMOUS

It's important to be a self-starter. Nobody is going to wind you up in the morning and give you a pep talk and push you out. You have to have a firm faith and belief in yourself.
LOU HOLTZ

# Opportunity

Opportunity seems to strike at the door of only those men who have prepared themselves for greater things.
CAPTAIN M. RIOUX

Opportunity is missed by most people because it is dressed in overalls and looks like work.
THOMAS ALVA EDISON

Make the most of yourself by fanning the tiny spark of possibility within you into the flame of achievement.
ANONYMOUS

To make a fortune, some assistance from fate is essential. Ability alone is insufficient.
IHARA SAIKAKU

Learn to listen. Opportunity sometimes knocks very softly.
ANONYMOUS

A wise man will make more opportunities than he finds.
SIR FRANCIS BACON

If you fail, it's because you took a chance; if you succeed, it's because you grasped an opportunity.
ANONYMOUS

A throw of the dice will never eliminate chance.
STÉPHANE MALLARMÉ

Remember that not getting what you want is sometimes a wonderful stroke of luck.
ANONYMOUS

Chance is always powerful. Let your hook be always cast. In the pool where you least expect it will be a fish.
OVID

A missed opportunity is never lost, for each time I drop one, somebody else picks it up.
ANONYMOUS

Believe in fate, but lean forward where fate can see you.
QUENTIN CRISP

# Opportunity

The golden opportunity you are seeking is in yourself. It is not in your environment, not in luck or chance, or the help of others; it is in yourself alone.
ANONYMOUS

In the middle of difficulty lies opportunity.
ALBERT EINSTEIN

If you don't pick up the ball and run with it… someone else will.
ANONYMOUS

Each man is the architect of his own destiny.
APPIUS CLAUDIUS CAECUS

Winners do not count on breaks; they make breaks count.
ANONYMOUS

Every man is the maker of his own fortune.
SIR RICHARD STEELE

Luck is when preparation meets opportunity.
ANONYMOUS

Ability is nothing without opportunity.
NAPOLEON BONAPARTE

An optimist sees an opportunity in every catastrophe. A pessimist sees a catastrophe in every opportunity.
ANONYMOUS

Do not suppose opportunity will knock twice at your door.
CHAMFORT

The trouble with opportunity is that it always comes disguised as hard work.
ANONYMOUS

They, believe me, who await
No gifts from chance, have conquered fate.
MATTHEW ARNOLD

Four things never come back—the spoken word, the sped arrow, the past life, and the neglected opportunity.
ANONYMOUS

# Persistence

Defeat doesn't finish a man – quit does. A man is not finished when he's defeated. He's finished when he quits.
RICHARD NIXON

It's not whether you get knocked down. It's whether you get up again.
VINCE LOMBARDI

Life is like riding a bicycle. You don't fall off unless you stop pedalling.
CLAUDE PEPPER

The race is not always to the swift, but to those who keep running.
ANONYMOUS

Go the extra mile. It's never crowded.
EXECUTIVE SPEEDWRITER NEWSLETTER

You ask, what is our aim? I can answer that in one word: victory at all costs, victory in spite of all terror, victory however long and hard the road may be; for without victory there is no survival.
WINSTON CHURCHILL

Top cats often begin as underdogs.
BERNARD MELTZER

In competition, nothing is *less* important than the score at halftime.
ANONYMOUS

The drop of rain maketh a hole in the stone, not by violence, but by oft falling.
BISHOP HUGH LATIMER

A man can do only what he can do. But if he does that each day, he can sleep at night and do it again the next day.
ALBERT SCHWEITZER

Let us, then, be up and doing,
With a heart for any fate;
Still achieving, still pursuing,
Learn to labour and to wait.
HENRY WADSWORTH LONGFELLOW

Fire your gun, then get ready to fire again, instead of talking about the first shot.
ANONYMOUS

# Persistence

A man of destiny knows that beyond this hill lies another and another. The journey is never complete.
F. W. De Klerk

Do what you can, with what you have, where you are.
Theodore Roosevelt

It's going to be a long, hard drag, but we'll make it.
Janis Joplin

Morale is when your hands and feet keep working when your head says it can't be done.
Anonymous

Man is not made for defeat. A man can be destroyed but not defeated.
Ernest Hemingway

That which we persist in doing becomes easier – not that the nature of the task has changed, but our ability to do has increased.
Ralph Waldo Emerson

They won because they refused to become discouraged by their defeats.
ANONYMOUS

A hero is one who knows how to hang on one minute longer.
NORWEGIAN PROVERB

Paralyze their resistance with your persistence.
ANONYMOUS

It is better to burn out than to fade away.
NEIL YOUNG

If people feel they have control over their destinies they will persist at tasks.
TOM PETERS AND ROBERT WATERMAN

From small beginnings come great things.
PROVERB

Persistence prevails when all else fails.
ANONYMOUS

# Persistence

Give in and you will never win.
ANONYMOUS

Even if tomorrow I knew the world would go to pieces I would still plant my apple tree.
MARTIN LUTHER

You may trod me in the very dirt
But still, like dust, I'll rise.
MAYA ANGELOU

No man is defeated without until he has first been defeated within.
ELEANOR ROOSEVELT

Failure is the line of least persistence.
ANONYMOUS

Press on. Nothing can take the place of persistence. Talent will not; nothing is more common than unsuccessful men with talent. Genius will not; the world is full of educated derelicts. Perseverance and determination alone are omnipotent.
CALVIN COOLIDGE

You just can't beat the person who never gives up.
BABE RUTH

What comes around usually comes around again to those who wait.
ANONYMOUS

Our greatest glory is not in never falling, but in rising every time we fall.
CONFUCIUS

The strength of the brave is to get up when you fall.
FRENCH PROVERB

Consider the postage stamp – its usefulness consists on the ability to stick to one thing till it gets there.
JOSH BILLINGS

We may encounter many defeats but we must not be defeated.
MAYA ANGELOU

# *Practice*

It takes twenty years to become an overnight success.
EDDIE CANTOR

For every pass I ever caught in a game, I caught a thousand in practice.
DON HUSTON

A minute lost in practice is never found.
ANONYMOUS

All our talents increase in the using, and every faculty, both good and bad, strengthens by exercise.
ANNE BRONTË

The great crises of life are not, I think, necessarily those which are in themselves the hardest to bear, but those for which we are least prepared.
MARY ADAMS

A genius is a talented person who does his homework.
THOMAS ALVA EDISON

Practice makes perfect, so be careful what you practice.
ANONYMOUS

Practice is the best of all instructors.
PUBLILIUS SYRUS

Practice without improvement is meaningless.
CHUCK KNOX

Decide today to plan and act for the long term. Practice short-term pain for long-term gain. And remember, the long view sharpens the short view.
ANONYMOUS

By nature, men are really alike; by practice, they get to be wide apart.
CONFUCIUS

One must learn by doing the thing; though you think you know it, you have no certainty until you try.
SOPHOCLES

# *Practice*

Steps to success: practice, work, sweat, achieve, shower, repeat.
ANONYMOUS

To be defeated is pardonable; to be surprised – never!
NAPOLEON BONAPARTE

Labour conquers all things.
VIRGIL

Man is born to labour, as a bird to fly.
PIUS XI

A gem cannot be polished without friction, nor man perfected without trials.
ANONYMOUS

Do not tell me how hard you work. Tell me how much you get done.
JAMES J. LING

You play the way you practice.
POP WARNER

You never get a second chance to make a good first impression.
ANONYMOUS

We cannot train without planning and we cannot teach without preparation.
GEORGE C. MARSHALL

The will to prepare to win is infinitely more important than the will to win. A team that is really willing to prepare is the team that has the best chance to win and wants to win.
BOBBY KNIGHT

The will to win is worthless if you do not have the will to prepare.
ANONYMOUS

Genius is one percent inspiration and ninety-nine percent perspiration.
THOMAS ALVA EDISON

Work: The doing is as important as what gets done, the making as valuable as the made.
THEODORE ROSZAK

# *Practice*

Practice does not make perfect. Perfect practice makes perfect.
ANONYMOUS

He who would leap high must take a long run.
DANISH PROVERB

Practice yourself… in little things; and thence proceed to greater.
EPICTETUS

Be a champion in practice. That is where champions are made.
ANONYMOUS

To be prepared is half the victory.
MIGUEL DE CERVANTES

You don't win football games on optimism. You win with preparation.
MONTE CLARK

Chance favours the prepared mind.
LOUIS PASTEUR

Sharpness in fundamentals is the winning edge.
ANONYMOUS

Failure to prepare certainly means preparing to fall.
JOHN WOODEN

The distance is nothing – it is only the first step that counts.
MARQUISE DU DEFFANT

The difference between good and great is taking care of the little things.
ANONYMOUS

Habit becomes a kind of second nature which acts as a motive for many of our actions.
MARCUS TULLIUS CICERO

The one unbreakable rule about hitting is this: if a batter hits well with his particular stance and swing, think twice—or more—before suggesting a change.
STAN MUSIAL

# Practice

Dig a well before you are thirsty.
ANONYMOUS

There's no such thing as natural touch. Touch is something you create by hitting millions of golf balls.
LEE TREVINO

You hit home runs not by chance, but by preparation.
ROGER MARIS

Remember the five P's: proper preparation prevents poor performance.
ANONYMOUS

Don't mistake activity for achievement— practice the right way.
JOHN WOODEN

The only thing that endures over time is the 'law of the farm.' You must prepare the ground, plant the seed, cultivate, and water if you expect to reap the harvest.
STEPHEN R. COVEY

I will get ready, and then perhaps my chance will come.
ABRAHAM LINCOLN


To win, a team has to be obsessive about the fundamentals and the little things.
JOE GIBBS


Spectacular success is preceded by spectacular, although invisible, mental preparation.
ANONYMOUS


Everyone has the will to win, but few have the will to prepare to win.
BOBBY KNIGHT


In all things, success depends upon previous preparation, and without such preparation there is sure to be failure.
CONFUCIUS

# *Success*

The secret of business is to know something that nobody else knows.
ARISTOTLE ONASSIS

You can win and still not succeed, still not achieve what you should. And you can lose without really failing at all.
BOBBY KNIGHT

The key to success isn't much good until one discovers the right lock to insert it in.
TEHYI HSIEH

Success depends on backbone, not wishbone.
ANONYMOUS

Success is a state of mind. If you want success, start thinking of yourself as a success.
JOYCE BROTHERS

The most important single ingredient in the formula of success is the knack of getting along with people.
THEODORE ROOSEVELT

Losing isn't the worst thing that can happen... as long as it doesn't happen to you.
ANONYMOUS

Success is not so much achievement as achieving. Refuse to join the cautious crowd that plays not to lose—play to win.
DAVID J. MAHONEY

I don't know the key to success, but the key to failure is trying to please everybody.
BILL COSBY

Some of us will do our jobs well and some will not, but we will all be judged by one thing—the result.
ANONYMOUS

Live together like brothers and do business like strangers.
ARABIC PROVERB

Success is that old ABC—ability, breaks, and courage.
CHARLES LUCKMAN

# Success

Success is believing in what you are doing.
ANONYMOUS

He who does not hope to win has already lost.
JOSÉ JOAQUÍN OLMEDO

… skate to where the puck is going to be, not where it has been.
WAYNE GRETZKY

Success is to be measured not so much by the position that one has reached as by the obstacles that one has overcome while trying to succeed.
MARK TWAIN

A winner respects those who are superior to him and tries to learn something from them; a loser resents those who are superior to him and tries to find chinks in their armour.
ANONYMOUS

Some are born great, some achieve greatness, and some hire public relations writers.
DANIEL J. BOORSTIN

For it is commonly said: 'Hard tasks are pleasant when they are finished.'
MARCUS TULLIUS CICERO

A winner feels responsible for more than his job; a loser says, "I only work here."
ANONYMOUS

To succeed in the world we do all we can do to appear successful.
FRANÇOIS DE LA ROCHEFOUCAULD

A minute's success pays the failure of years.
ROBERT BROWNING

A winner knows what to fight for and what to compromise on; a loser compromises on what he shouldn't and fights for what isn't worthwhile fighting about.
ANONYMOUS

Of course I don't look busy; I did it right the first time.
SCOTT ADAMS

# Success

Victory has a thousand fathers but defeat is an orphan.
JOHN F. KENNEDY

A winner credits good luck for winning, even though it isn't good luck. A loser blames bad luck for losing even though it isn't bad luck.
ANONYMOUS

Sometimes something worth doing is worth overdoing.
DAVID LETTERMAN

An expert is a man who has made all the mistakes which can be made in a very narrow field.
NIELS HENRIK DAVID BOHR

A winner works harder than a loser and has more time; a loser is always too busy to do what is necessary.
ANONYMOUS

We are taught by great actions that the universe is the property of every individual in it.
RALPH WALDO EMERSON

Few people do business well who do nothing else.
LORD CHESTERFIELD


Success, as I see it, is a result, not a goal.
GUSTAVE FLAUBERT


A winner goes through a problem; a loser goes around it and never past it.
ANONYMOUS


If you wish in this world to advance
Your merits you're bound to enhance,
You must stir it and stump it,
And blow your own trumpet,
Or, trust me, you haven't a chance!
W. S. GILBERT


The reward of a thing well done, is to have done it.
RALPH WALDO EMERSON


Judge your success by what you had to give up in order to get it.
ANONYMOUS

# *Success*

Success is a matter of luck, ask any failure.
EARL WILSON

Over the years, I have become convinced that every detail is important and that success usually accompanies attention to little details. It is this, in my judgment, that makes for the difference between champion and near champion.
JOHN WOODEN

Winning is a habit. Unfortunately, so is losing.
ANONYMOUS

The ability to convert ideas to things is the secret of outward success.
HENRY WARD BEECHER

Nothing is illegal if one hundred businessmen decide to do it.
ANDREW YOUNG

The road to success is always under construction.
ANONYMOUS

Two people in the same business on the same street. One of them prospers and the other does not. Why? Because one of them wants it more than the other. It is not always the strongest man who wins the fight, or the fastest man who wins the race, or the best team that wins the game. In most cases it is the one who wants it the most, the one who has gone out and prepared, who has paid the price.
TOMMY LASORDA

I have taken great care not to laugh at human actions, not to weep at them, nor to hate them, but to understand them.
BARUCH SPINOZA

A winner paces himself; losers go fast or slow.
ANONYMOUS

A successful coach is one who is still coaching.
BEN SCHWARTZWALDER

Every time you win, you're reborn; when you lose, you die a little.
GEORGE ALLEN

If you have an important point to make, don't try to be subtle or clever. Use a pile-driver. Hit the point once. Then come back and hit it a second time – a tremendous whack!
WINSTON CHURCHILL

Success, at any level, depends on the ability to pick the right people for the right jobs.
ANONYMOUS

Only a mediocre person is always at his best.
SOMERSET MAUGHAM

There is no merit in equality, unless it be equality with the best.
JOHN LANCASTER SPALDING

If you are average, you are as close to the bottom as you are to the top.
ANONYMOUS

If we did all the things we are capable of doing, we would literally astound ourselves.
THOMAS ALVA EDISON

Only through experience of trial and suffering can the soul be strengthened, vision cleared, ambition inspired, and success achieved.
HELEN KELLER

To be average is to be the lowest of the good and the best of the bad.
ANONYMOUS

Success is a fickle jade. The clothes on her back may be put there by hard work, but her jewels are the gifts of chance.
SIR CHARLES WHEELER

Old age is like everything else. To make a success of it, you've got to start young.
FRED ASTAIRE

Show me a good and gracious loser, and I'll show you a failure.
KNUTE ROCKNE

You can't keep a good man down or a bad man up.
P. K. THOMAJAN

# Success

Give the world the best you have and the best will come back to you.
ANONYMOUS

We judge ourselves by what we feel capable of doing, while others judge us by what we have already done.
HENRY WADSWORTH LONGFELLOW

To be what we are, and to become what we are capable of becoming, is the only end in life.
BARUCH SPINOZA

Fame is what others give you. Success is what you give yourself.
ANONYMOUS

Destiny is not a matter of chance, it is a matter of choice; it is not a thing to be waited for, it is a thing to be achieved.
WILLIAM JENNINGS BRYAN

It is no use saying, "We are doing our best." You have got to succeed in doing what is necessary.
WINSTON CHURCHILL

Thinking always of trying to do more brings a state of mind in which nothing seems impossible.
HENRY FORD

A winner listens; a loser just waits until it is his turn to talk.
ANONYMOUS

A lifetime contract for a coach means, if you're ahead at the third quarter, moving the ball, they can't fire you.
LOU HOLTZ

Winning is everything. The only ones who remember when you come second are your wife and your dog.
DAMON HILL

Are you trying to make something *for* yourself or something *of* yourself?
ANONYMOUS

When love and skill work together, expect a masterpiece.
JOHN RUSKIN

# Success

The toughest thing about success is that you've got to keep on being a success. Talent is only a starting point in this business. You've got to keep on working that talent.
IRVING BERLIN

True success is the only thing you cannot have unless and until you have offered it to others.
ANONYMOUS

There's only one surefire way to succeed in business: make something people want, make it well, and make it in one size.
HENRY FORD

My grandfather once told me that there are two kinds of people: those who do the work and those who take the credit. He told me to try to be in the first group; there was less competition there.
INDIRA GANDHI

The secret of success: 1) get a job; 2) get a better job; 3) get an even better job; 4) repeat as often as necessary.
MATT GROENING

Success consists of doing the common things uncommonly well.
ANONYMOUS

The fastest way to succeed is to look as if you're playing by other people's rules, while quietly playing by your own.
MICHAEL KORDA

One thing common to most success stories is the alarm clock.
ANONYMOUS

Pile it high, sell it cheap.
SIR JACK COHEN

If you can react the same way to winning and losing, that… quality is important because it stays with you the rest of your life.
CHRIS EVERT

The best teams try to fix things when they're winning, not after they start to lose.
KEVIN CONSTANTINE

# Teamwork

Coming together is a beginning; keeping together is progress; working together is success.
HENRY FORD

One man can be a crucial ingredient on a team, but one man cannot make a team.
KAREEM ABDUL-JABBAR

When you come to practice, you cease to exist as an individual. You're part of a team.
JOHN WOODEN

Have faith in teammates. Believe in them, trust them, and you will draw out the best in them. They will rise high to your expectations.
ANONYMOUS

Nothing is impossible for the man who does not have to do it himself.
EARL WILSON

We must have infinite faith in each other. If we have not, we must never let it leak out that we have not.
HENRY DAVID THOREAU

Are you playing for your name in the paper, or your name on the trophy?
SHERRY BASSIN

Equal opportunity for all, special privileges for none.
ANONYMOUS

To be a team and united as one is a great achievement; yet to respect the right to be an individual may be even greater.
MICHAEL VESIA

It's easy to get good players. Getting 'em to play together, that's the hard part.
CASEY STENGEL

You can run the office without a boss, but you can't run an office without the secretaries.
JANE FONDA

The way to get things done is not to mind who gets the credit for doing them.
BENJAMIN JOWETT

# Teamwork

Teamwork is the fuel that allows common people to attain uncommon results.
ANONYMOUS

Union gives strength.
AESOP

Unity and confidence cannot be improvised. They alone can create that mutual trust, that feeling of force which gives courage and daring.
ARDANT DU PICQ

The secret of winning football games is working more as a team, less as individuals. I play not my 11 best, but my best 11.
KNUTE ROCKNE

The amount that can be controlled and executed by a team is controlled by the weakest man on it.
ANONYMOUS

The way a team plays as a whole determines its success.
BABE RUTH

There's no letter 'I' in the word teamwork.
BILL FOSTER

You may be on top of the heap, but remember, you are still part of it.
ANONYMOUS

It is my belief that discipline, well-earned pride, and a high-degree of unselfishness contribute to achieving a desirable morale… the most important element in a successful team.
JOHN MAJORS

In order to have a winner, the team must have a feeling of unity; every player must put the team first, ahead of personal glory.
PAUL 'BEAR' BRYANT

It is literally true that you can succeed best and quickest by helping others to succeed.
NAPOLEON HILL

Behind an able man there are always other able men.
CHINESE PROVERB

# Teamwork

Our titles would not have been possible without the unselfishness displayed by all our teams; the team wins, not the individuals.
JOHN WOODEN

Teamwork is the ability to work together toward a common vision, the ability to direct individual accomplishment toward organizational objectives. It is the fuel that allows common people to attain uncommon results.
ANONYMOUS

I like to have a closely-knit team. I like players to do things together off the court. I like to show them I care about their problems. I want them to know that they and winning come first.
BOB COUSY

Are you playing for the name on the back of your sweater or the name on the front of the sweater?
SHERRY BASSIN

Teamwork divides the tasks and doubles the successes.
ANONYMOUS

Larry Bird is one hell of a competitor. You can tell he's hurting, he's not running as well as he should, he's pulling back. But you say, "Larry, are you alright?" and he says, "Yeah," and goes out there and does his job. Those are the kind of guys you go across the river with, guys you go over the mountain with. I've never known another player so loyal. If you're Larry's teammate, you're one of the most important people in the world to him.
KEVIN MCHALE

Harmony makes small things grow; lack of it makes great things decay.
SALLUST

Teamwork is the collective talents of many individuals.
ANONYMOUS

It's amazing what a team can accomplish when no one cares who gets the credit.
JOHN WOODEN

Together we shall achieve victory.
DWIGHT D. EISENHOWER

# Teamwork

**T**ogether
**E**veryone
**A**chieves
**M**ore

ANONYMOUS

**B**y union the smallest states thrive. By discord the greatest are destroyed.

SALLUST

**B**eing together as a team is more important than winning. If you're not together as a team, any success you have is not going to last. Achieve togetherness, achieve unity of purpose, and success will follow.

PAT RILEY

**H**e who wished to secure the good of others, has already secured his own.

CONFUCIUS

**N**o problem is insurmountable. With a little courage, teamwork, and determination, a person can overcome anything.

B. DODGE

The nice thing about teamwork is that you always have others on your side.
MARGARET CARTY

Everybody on a championship team doesn't get publicity, but everyone can say he's a champion.
EARVIN 'MAGIC' JOHNSON

Alone we can do so little; together we can do so much.
HELEN KELLER

Many hands make light work.
JOHN HEYWOOD

If a team is to reach its potential, each player must be willing to subordinate his personal goals to the good of the team.
BUD WILKINSON

Teamwork means success – work together, win together.
ANONYMOUS

# Time

Adopt the pace of nature: her secret is patience.
RALPH WALDO EMERSON

The world is moving so fast these days that the man who says it can't be done, is generally interrupted by someone doing it.
ELBERT HUBBARD

Those who watch the clock won't need to worry about their future—they won't have any.
ANONYMOUS

I never think of the future. It comes soon enough.
ALBERT EINSTEIN

Half our life is spent trying to find something to do with the time we have rushed through life trying to save.
WILL ROGERS

A meeting is an event where the minutes are kept and the hours are lost.
ANONYMOUS

Time heals what reason cannot.

LUCIUS ANNAEUS SENECA

Nine-tenths of wisdom is being wise in time.

THEODORE ROOSEVELT

Men talk of killing time, while time quietly kills them.

DION BOUCICAULT

I always wanted to be a procrastinator, but I never got around to it.

ANONYMOUS

Today's greatest labour-saving device is tomorrow.

TOM WILSON

Those who make the worst use of their time are the first to complain of its brevity.

JEAN DE LA BRUYÈRE

Time brings everything.

PLATO

# Time

Time goes, you say? Ah no!
Alas, Time stays, we go.
HENRY AUSTIN DOBSON

You must learn to separate the urgent from
the important. The important is rarely urgent, and the
urgent is rarely important.
ANONYMOUS

There is no past, present, or future. Using
tenses to divide time is like making chalk marks
over water.
JANET FRAME

There is more to life than increasing its
speed.
MOHANDAS K. GANDHI

Procrastination is the art of keeping up with
yesterday.
ANONYMOUS

The years teach much that the days never
know.
RALPH WALDO EMERSON

Perfection is the child of Time.
JOSEPH HALL

It may be true that preoccupation with time
has been the downfall of Western man, but it can
also be argued that conjecture about eternity is a
waste of time.
QUENTIN CRISP

A procrastinator's work is never done.
ANONYMOUS

Never put off till tomorrow what you can do
today.
PROVERB

This is not the end, it is not even the
beginning of the end, but is perhaps the end of the
beginning.
WINSTON CHURCHILL

Change is the law of life. And those who
look only to the past or the present are certain to
miss the future.
JOHN F. KENNEDY

# *Time*

**N**ot 'managing' your time, but mastering you time. There's a great difference.
ANONYMOUS

**Y**ou can't measure time in days the way you can money in dollars because every day is different.
JORGE LUIS BORGES

**T**here is nothing so useless as doing efficiently that which should not be done at all.
PETER F. DRUCKER

**T**ime is neutral with a bias in favour of the side that exhibits the more intelligent initiative.
REGINALD HARGREAVES

**T**he sooner you fall behind, the more time you'll have to catch up.
ANONYMOUS

**I** think time is a merciless thing. I think life is a process of burning oneself out and time is the fire that burns you. But I think the spirit of man is a good adversary.
TENNESSEE WILLIAMS

He who gains time gains everything.

BENJAMIN DISRAELI

It is even better to act quickly and err than to hesitate until the time of action is past.

KARL VON CLAUSEWITZ

Don't count the days, make the days count.

ANONYMOUS

Who controls the past controls the future. Who controls the present controls the past.

GEORGE ORWELL

The present is the ever-moving shadow that divides yesterday from tomorrow. In that lies hope.

FRANK LLOYD WRIGHT

Chance is the only thing you can't buy.... You have to pay for it and you have to pay for it with your life, spending a lot of time, you pay for it with time – not the wasting of time, but the spending of time.

ROBERT DOISNEAU

# Time

Each day we are given a valuable gift, a 'new day.' What will we do with that gift? The choice is ours to make good use of it or squander it.
ANONYMOUS

I haven't got time to be tired.
WILHELM I

We live in a moment of history where change is so speeded up that we begin to see the present only when it is already disappearing.
R. D. LAING

Do you value life? Then waste not time, for that is the stuff of which life is made.
BENJAMIN FRANKLIN

Yesterday is a cancelled check; tomorrow is a promissory note; today is the only cash you have. Spend it wisely!
ANONYMOUS

I recommend to you to take care of minutes; for hours will take care of themselves.
LORD CHESTERFIELD

The best thing about the future is that it comes only one day at a time.
ABRAHAM LINCOLN

Make hay while the sun shines.
ENGLISH PROVERB

What you do tomorrow will never make up for what you lost today.
ANONYMOUS

Time deals gently only with those who take it gently.
ANATOLE FRANCE

Be quick, but never hurry.
JOHN WOODEN

The biggest sin in life is wasting time.
ANONYMOUS

Remember that time is money.
BENJAMIN FRANKLIN

# Time

Time ripens all things. No man's born wise.
MIGUEL DE CERVANTES

Don't use time or words carelessly. Neither can be retrieved.
ANONYMOUS

But at my back I always hear time's wingèd chariot hurrying near.
ANDREW MARVELL

There is one kind of robber whom the law does not strike at, and who steals what is most precious to men – time.
NAPOLEON I

If you don't take the time to do it right, will you have the time to do it over?
ANONYMOUS

Time is not the fourth dimension, and should not be so identified. Time is only a relative observation.
BUCKMINSTER FULLER

One always has time enough, if only one applies it well.
JOHANN WOLFGANG VON GOETHE

Time is a merciless enemy, as it is also a merciless friend and healer.
MOHANDAS K. GANDHI

Counting time is not so important as making time count.
ANONYMOUS

You may delay, but time will not.
BENJAMIN FRANKLIN

Everything happens to everybody sooner or later if there is time enough.
GEORGE BERNARD SHAW

We must use time wisely, and forever realize that the time is always ripe to do right.
NELSON MANDELA

# *Vision*

The length of my walk is the length of my thought.
HENRY DAVID THOREAU

Cherish your visions and your dreams as they are the children of your soul; the blueprints of your ultimate achievements.
NAPOLEON HILL

Whatever you can do, or dream you can, begin it. Boldness has genius, power, and magic in it.
JOHANN WOLFGANG VON GOETHE

Champion the right to be yourself; dare to be different and set your own pattern; live your own life and follow your own star.
ANONYMOUS

Let us not go over the old ground, let us rather prepare for what is to come.
MARCUS TULLIUS CICERO

Dream, diversify – and never miss an angle.
WALT DISNEY

Winners see what they want to happen. Losers see what they want to avoid.
ANONYMOUS

When you sleep, you don't control your dream. I like to dive into a dream world that I've made, a world I chose and that I have complete control over.
DAVID LYNCH

What man can imagine, he may one day achieve.
NANCY HALE

Probable impossibilities are always to be preferred to improbable possibilities.
ARISTOTLE

What your mind can conceive and your heart can believe, your body can achieve.
ANONYMOUS

We've removed the ceiling above our dreams. There are no more impossible dreams.
JESSE JACKSON

# Vision

**D**reams come true; without that possibility, nature would not incite us to have them.
JOHN UPDIKE

**W**hat we call luck is the inner man externalized. We make things happen to us.
ROBERTSON DAVIES

**H**appy are those who dream dreams and are ready to pay the price to make them come true.
ANONYMOUS

**M**y interest is in the future because I'm going to spend the rest of my life there.
CHARLES KETTERING

**I**magination is more important than knowledge.
ALBERT EINSTEIN

**I**t takes a little talent to see clearly what lies under one's nose, a good deal of it to know in which direction to point that organ.
W. H. AUDEN

If you can imagine it, you can achieve it. If you can dream it, you can become it.
ANONYMOUS

The only limits, as always, are those of vision.
JAMES BROUGHTON

I like the dreams of the future better than the history of the past.
THOMAS JEFFERSON

The future belongs to those that believe in the beauty of their dreams.
ELEANOR ROOSEVELT

Throw your heart over the bar and your body will follow.
ANONYMOUS

When you reach for the stars, you may not quite get one, but you won't come up with a handful of mud either.
LEO BURNETT

# *Vision*

Climb every mountain, ford every stream, follow every rainbow till you find your dream.
OSCAR HAMMERSTEIN II

He who has heart has hope, and he who has hope has everything.
ARABIAN PROVERB

Success is a dream turned into reality.
ANONYMOUS

If a man wants his dream to come true, he must wake up.
HERBERT PROCHNOW

The trouble with our times is that the future is not what it used to be.
PAUL VALÉRY

Hitch your wagon to a star.
RALPH WALDO EMERSON

Dream what you dare to dream. Go where you want to go. Be what you want to be.
ANONYMOUS

We understand things by means of what we do. That is to say, without doing something we tend to be blind to everything. But the moment we do do something, that action opens our vision to the things in the past and the things in the future.
JOHN CAGE


To be what we are, and to become what we are capable of becoming, is the only end of life.
ROBERT LOUIS STEVENSON


Nothing ever built arose to touch the skies unless some man dreamed that it should, some man believed that it could, and some man willed that it must.
CHARLES KETTERING


Dream more than others think is practical; expect more than others think is possible.
ANONYMOUS


If you don't dream, you may as well be dead.
GEORGE FOREMAN

# Wisdom

The wise man is not the man who gives the right answers; he is the one who asks the right questions.
CLAUDE LÉVIS-STRAUSS

Nothing in life is to be feared. It is only to be understood.
MARIE CURIE

The art of being wise is the art of knowing what to overlook.
WILLIAM JAMES

Small minds discuss people. Average minds discuss events. Great minds discuss ideas.
ANONYMOUS

It is the province of knowledge to speak and it is the privilege of wisdom to listen.
OLIVER WENDELL HOLMES

There are two things to aim at in life: first, to get what you want; and after that, to enjoy it. Only the wisest of mankind achieve the second.
LOGAN PEARSALL SMITH

Honesty is the first chapter of the book of wisdom.
THOMAS JEFFERSON


Genius is patience.
COMTE DE BUFFON


Authority without wisdom is like a heavy ax without an edge, fitter to bruise than polish.
ANNE BRADSTREET


Praise in public, criticize in private.
ANONYMOUS


It is better to know some of the questions than all of the answers.
JAMES THURBER


Never ruin an apology with an excuse.
KIMBERLY JOHNSON


If you are patient in one moment of anger, you will escape a hundred days of sorrow.
CHINESE PROVERB

# Wisdom

**A**nger is never without a reason, but seldom with a good one.
BENJAMIN FRANKLIN

**S**ometimes the road less travelled is less travelled for a reason.
JERRY SEINFELD

**W**hen you're in it up to your ears, you should keep your mouth shut.
ANONYMOUS

**T**he stupid neither forgive nor forget; the naïve forgive and forget; the wise forgive but do not forget.
THOMAS SZASZ

**B**e wiser than other people if you can; but do not tell them so.
LORD CHESTERFIELD

**W**hen you have got an elephant by the hind leg, and he is trying to run away, it's best to let him run.
ABRAHAM LINCOLN

May you have the hindsight to know where you've been, the foresight to know where you're going, and the insight to know when you've gone too far.

ANONYMOUS

To have made a beginning is half of the business; dare to be wise.

HORACE

Some folks are wise, and some are otherwise.

TOBIAS SMOLLETT

Never wrestle a pig. You both get dirty and the pig enjoys it.

ANONYMOUS

One may learn wisdom even from one's enemies.

ARISTOPHANES

It is a characteristic of wisdom not to do desperate things.

HENRY DAVID THOREAU

# Wisdom

Experience is the mother of wisdom.
PROVERB

Believe only half of what you see and nothing that you hear.
DINAH MULOCK CRAIK

When your work speaks for itself, do not interrupt.
ANONYMOUS

He that walketh with wise men shall be wise....
BIBLE, PROVERBS 13:20

The truth is more important than the facts.
FRANK LLOYD WRIGHT

A moment's insight is sometimes worth a life's experience.
OLIVER WENDELL HOLMES

Even he who is wiser than the wise may err.
AESCHYLUS

For every action, there is an equal and opposite criticism.
ANONYMOUS

Wise living consists perhaps less in acquiring good habits than in acquiring as few habits as possible.
ERIC HOFFER

It is not that you do wrong by design, but that you should never do right by mistake.
JUNIUS

A man should never be ashamed to own he has been in the wrong, which is but saying, in other words, that he is wiser today than he was yesterday.
ALEXANDER POPE

The heart of the wise, like a mirror, should reflect all objects without being sullied by any.
CONFUCIUS

It is much easier to be critical than to be correct.
BENJAMIN DISRAELI

# *Wisdom*

Remember that silence is sometimes the best answer.
ANONYMOUS

When everyone is wrong, everyone is right.
NIVELLE DE LA CHAUSSÉE

For one word a man is often deemed to be wise, and for one word he is often deemed to be foolish. We should be careful indeed what we say.
CONFUCIUS

Talking and eloquence are not the same; to speak, and to speak well, are two things.
BEN JONSON

A man's body and his mind… are exactly like a jerkin and a jerkin's lining – rumple the one, you rumple the other.
LAURENCE STERNE

Don't tell other people your troubles. Half of them aren't interested, and the other half are glad you got what you had coming to you.
ANONYMOUS

The wisest man sometimes acts weakly, and the weakest sometimes wisely.
LORD CHESTERFIELD

When you know a thing, to hold that you know it, and when you do not know it, to admit that you do not – this is true knowledge.
CONFUCIUS

There are three things that ought to be considered before some things are spoken – the manner, the place, and the time.
ROBERT SOUTHEY

Important principles may and must be flexible.
ABRAHAM LINCOLN

The best way to save face is to keep the lower part shut.
ANONYMOUS

Good actions ennoble us, and we are the sons of our own deeds.
MIGUEL DE CERVANTES

# Wisdom

It is easier to be wise on behalf of others than to be so for ourselves.

FRANÇOIS DE LA ROCHEFOUCAULD

The more extensive a man's knowledge of what has been done, the greater will be his power of knowing what to do.

BENJAMIN DISRAELI

It is best to remain silent and be thought of as a fool than to speak up and remove all doubt.

ABRAHAM LINCOLN

Every man values himself more than all the rest of men, but he always values others' opinion of himself more than his own.

MARCUS AURELIUS ANTONINUS

Excuses are like belly buttons—everybody has one.

ANONYMOUS

Men do not stumble over mountains, but over molehills.

CONFUCIUS

Always remember that when you are in the right you can afford to keep your temper, and when you are in the wrong you cannot afford to lose it.
JOHN J. REYNOLDS

What you do speaks so loud I can't hear what you say.
RALPH WALDO EMERSON

When all is said and done, as a rule, more is said than done.
LOU HOLTZ

The longest distance between two points is a short-cut.
ANONYMOUS

They must often change who would be constant in happiness or wisdom.
CONFUCIUS

Be nice to people on your way up because you'll need them on your way down.
WILSON MIZNER

# Wisdom

**R**espect yourself and others will respect you.
CONFUCIUS

**A** wise man turns chance into good fortune.
THOMAS FULLER

**F**ixing the problem is more important than affixing the blame.
ANONYMOUS

**L**end only what you can afford to lose.
PROVERB

**P**atience is the companion of wisdom.
SAINT AUGUSTINE

**W**isdom consists not so much in knowing what to do in the ultimate as in knowing what to do next.
HERBERT HOOVER

**P**eople who jump to conclusions generally leap over the facts.
ANONYMOUS

Nine-tenths of wisdom is being wise in time.
THEODORE ROOSEVELT

No enemy is worse than bad advice.
SOPHOCLES

Judge a man by his questions rather than by his answers.
VOLTAIRE

Knowledge itself is power.
SIR FRANCIS BACON

Advice is like castor oil – easy enough to give, but difficult to take.
ANONYMOUS

Nothing is permanent but change.
HERACLITUS

The great thing about getting older is that you don't lose all the other ages you've been.
MADELEINE L'ENGLE

# Wisdom

Common sense is as rare as genius.
RALPH WALDO EMERSON

The business of finding fault is very easy, and that of doing better very difficult.
SAINT FRANCIS DE SALES

I acted, and my action made me wise.
THOM GUNN

Prepare and prevent instead of repair and repent.
ANONYMOUS

The most valuable of all talents is that of never using two words when one will do.
THOMAS JEFFERSON

What is the use of running when we are not on the right road?
GERMAN PROVERB

A closed mind is a dying mind.
EDNA FERBER

The thinker dies, but his thoughts are beyond the reach of destruction. Men are mortal; but ideas are immortal.

WALTER LIPPMANN

When giving advice, it's best to make it brief.

ANONYMOUS

The wise man is informed in what is right. The inferior man is informed in what will pay.

CONFUCIUS

History teaches us that men and nations behave wisely once they have exhausted all other alternatives.

ABBA EBAN

It is a characteristic of wisdom not to do desperate things.

HENRY DAVID THOREAU

The wise think what they say; the fools say what they think.

ANONYMOUS

# Wisdom

Nothing is opened by mistake as often as one's mouth.
ANONYMOUS

A mistake is simply another way of doing things.
KATHARINE GRAHAM

He who conquers others is strong; he who conquers himself is mighty.
LAO-TZU

Wisdom we know is the knowledge of good and evil – not the strength to choose between the two.
JOHN CHEEVER

Common sense is very uncommon.
HORACE GREELY

God grant me the serenity to accept the things that I cannot change, the courage to change the things I can, and the wisdom to know the difference.
REINHOLD NIEBUHR

Wisdom begins in wonder.
SOCRATES


The way I see it, if you want the rainbow,
you gotta put up with the rain.
DOLLY PARTON


When you can't change the direction of the
wind, adjust your sails.
ANONYMOUS


It requires wisdom to understand wisdom—
the music is nothing if the audience is deaf.
WALTER LIPPMAN


Wisdom is the reward you get for a lifetime
of listening when you would rather have talked.
MARK TWAIN


Always listen to experts. They'll tell you
what can't be done and why. Then do it.
ROBERT HEINLEN

# The ABCs of Achievement
## In Sport, Business, & Life

ATTITUDE… the foundation, the mark of you… keep yours POSITIVE

BELIEF… in your UNIQUE, capable self… you're a WINNER

COURAGE… to try, and to keep trying until you ACHIEVE YOUR GOALS

DISCIPLINE… it pays off in results… you must have it TO ACHIEVE

ENTHUSIASM…make it part of you and share it with others

FUN… it has to be there for meaningful results… MAKE ACHIEVING FUN

GOALS… your success targets AIM HIGH… and then HIGHER

Hope… the magic ingredient that sparks you into POSITIVE ACTION

Initiative… DO IT NOW! It pays off in results. IT'S DETERMINATION IN ACTION

Just… BE honourable and fair in *all* your dealings and actions

Knowledge… work hard to acquire it, but most of all, USE IT

Love… in all that you do… love MUST set the pace

Motivation… that which forces you into ACTION. It must be self-motivation for ACHIEVEMENT

Negatives… avoid them, keep them out of your environment, especially negative people

O<small>PTIMISM</small>… know you can… because Y<small>OU</small> C<small>AN DO IT</small>

P<small>RACTICE</small>… to succeed, you must practice-practice-practice

Q<small>UALITY AND</small> Q<small>UANTITY</small>… the twins of achievement, your calling cards as a person, as an A<small>CHIEVER</small>

R<small>ESPONSIBILITY</small>… doing the right thing because I<small>T'S THE RIGHT THING TO DO</small>

S<small>ELF-ESTEEM</small>… a P<small>OSITIVE SELF-IMAGE</small> is priceless—work on yours

T<small>OUGHNESS</small>… mental and physical—an unbeatable combination… G<small>O FOR IT</small>

U<small>NDERSTANDING</small>… know your strengths and weaknesses… A<small>CCENTUATE YOUR POSITIVES</small>

Virtue… the quality of moral excellence… it must be 'No. 1' in your LIVING PHILOSOPHY

Winning… your reward for HARD WORK and a POSITIVE ATTITUDE

Xtra mile… can't achieve without it… YOU HAVE TO WORK… WORK… WORK

You… THE MOST IMPORTANT INGREDIENT IN ACHIEVING YOUR SUCCESS

Zest… your GO-POWER. TURN IT ON AND LET IT FLOW

Make it happen in your life. It's as easy as A to Z.
Art Niemann

# Author Index